Google Pixel 9a User Guide

Master Every Feature with Easy Steps

Perfect for Beginners and Seniors, with Essential Tips and Tricks to Unlock Your Phone's Full Potential

RHODA DALY

Dedication

Dedicated to all those who embrace learning and technology with an open heart, and to those who help make the world a little bit easier for others—especially beginners and seniors   on their journey to mastering new skills.ok

Table of Contents

Chapter 1

Welcome to Your Google Pixel 9a

1.1 Introduction to the Pixel 9a

The **Google Pixel 9a** is more than just a smartphone; it's a tool designed to fit seamlessly into your daily life. With its sleek design, cutting-edge technology, and user-friendly interface, the Pixel 9a is built to elevate your mobile experience. Whether you're using it for work, entertainment, or simply staying connected, this device is packed with features that ensure it performs with ease. From the **Google Tensor G4 chip** to the innovative camera system, the Pixel 9a is designed to make your digital life more efficient, enjoyable, and secure. Get ready to explore the device that brings Google's best features to the palm of your hand.

1.2 Key Features at a Glance

- **48MP Main Camera**: Capture professional-quality photos with ease, even in low light, using advanced AI-powered tools like **Night Sight**.

- **Google Tensor G4 Chip**: Power through tasks effortlessly with a chip designed for speed and efficiency, keeping your apps and games running smoothly.

- **6.3" pOLED Display**: A stunning display with vibrant colors and deep contrasts that makes everything from streaming to browsing come to life.

- **Battery Life**: A 5,100mAh battery that keeps you going all day long, coupled with 23W fast charging and wireless charging options.

- **7 Years of Software Updates**: Stay ahead with Google's promise of consistent and long-term software support, ensuring your phone is always up to date.

- **Seamless Google Integration**: Enjoy exclusive features like **Google Assistant**, **Google Photos**, and **Google Lens**, all built into your device for a smart, connected experience.

1.3 Why This Guide is Perfect for You

This guide is designed with you in mind. Whether you're a **beginner** exploring your first smartphone or a **senior** looking for a device that's easy to use yet powerful, the Pixel 9a offers something for everyone. You'll find step-by-step instructions, **practical tips**, and **hidden features** that will help you get the most out of your phone, no matter your experience level. The goal of this guide is to make your Pixel 9a experience smooth and enjoyable. You don't need to be a tech expert to unlock its full potential. Let's dive in and make sure you're equipped to master your device with ease.

Chapter 2

Getting Started: Unbox and Set Up

2.1 What's in the Box

When you unbox your **Google Pixel 9a**, you'll find everything you need to get started right away. Here's a quick rundown of what's inside:

- **Google Pixel 9a Smartphone**: Your new device, sleek and ready for use, featuring a 6.3" pOLED display and all the powerful features you've been waiting for.

- **USB-C to USB-C Charging Cable**: For fast, efficient charging and data transfer. The USB-C connection ensures high-speed performance.

- **18W USB-C Charger**: This charger provides fast charging capabilities, so you can power up your Pixel 9a quickly and get back to what you love doing.

- **SIM Ejector Tool**: A small but essential tool for inserting or removing your SIM card easily.

- **Quick Start Guide**: A simple guide to help you get started with your new device, walking you through the initial setup and basic features.

- **Warranty Information**: Important details about your Pixel 9a's warranty, so you can ensure peace of mind as you start your journey with the device.

Everything is neatly packed to ensure you have a smooth, hassle-free setup experience. Once you've opened the box, you're just a few simple steps away from activating your new Google Pixel 9a and exploring its powerful features.

2.2 Setup for Beginners and Seniors

Setting up your **Google Pixel 9a** is quick and easy, even if you're new to smartphones or looking for a straightforward experience. Follow these simple steps to get your device up and running in no time:

1. **Power   On   Your   Pixel   9a**

    ○ Press and hold the **power button** located on the right side of the device until the Google logo appears on the screen. Your phone will power on and take you to the setup screen.

2. **Select   Your   Language**

    ○ The first screen you see will ask you to choose your **language**. Tap your preferred language and proceed.

3. Connect to Wi-Fi

- Next, you'll be prompted to **connect to a Wi-Fi network**. Select your Wi-Fi from the list and enter the password. This step will ensure your device can download any necessary updates during setup.

4. Sign in with Your Google Account

- You'll be asked to sign in to your **Google account**. If you already have one, simply enter your email and password. If you don't have a Google account, you can create one directly on this screen.

- Signing in ensures that your apps, photos, and other Google services are synced with your new device.

5. Set Up Your Fingerprint or Face Unlock

○ For added security, you can set up **fingerprint recognition** or **Face Unlock**. This allows you to easily unlock your phone with just a touch or a glance.

○ Follow the on-screen instructions to **register your fingerprint** or **set up facial recognition**.

6. Transfer Data (Optional)

○ If you're upgrading from another phone, Google will guide you through the process of transferring **your contacts, photos, and apps**. You can use a **cable** or **Wi-Fi** to move your data from your old phone to your Pixel 9a.

7. **Customize** **Your** **Settings**

- ○ You can choose your **theme**, adjust your **display settings**, and set up **notifications** in the **"Settings"** menu. Don't worry, you can always change these later if needed.

8. **Install** **Essential** **Apps**

- ○ Once you're set up, you can head over to the **Google Play Store** to download your favorite apps like social media, entertainment, or productivity tools.

Now your **Google Pixel 9a** is ready to use! With these simple steps, you've completed the basic setup, and you're all set to start exploring the many features of your new device. Whether you're a beginner or a senior, this guide will continue to walk you through every step to get the most out of your phone.

2.3 Personalizing Your Device

Now that your **Google Pixel 9a** is set up, it's time to make it truly yours by personalizing it to fit your style and preferences. With just a few easy steps, you can make your device more comfortable to use and uniquely yours.

1. **Change   Your   Wallpaper**

   ○ To change your wallpaper, **tap and hold** on an empty space on your home screen. Select **"Wallpaper & Style"** from the options. Choose from a range of **default wallpapers** or upload your own   photo.

   ○ You   can   also   set   **dynamic wallpapers**, which change throughout the day based on the time or weather.

2. **Set Up Themes and Display Preferences**

   ○ Under **"Wallpaper & Style"**, you can also adjust your **theme**. You can choose between **light** and **dark modes** to suit your preference or the time of day. Dark mode can save battery life and is gentler on the eyes, especially in low light.

○ Customize your **home screen layout** by choosing between a **grid size** that best fits your apps and widgets.

3. Organize Apps on Your Home Screen

○ For easy access to the apps you use most, drag and drop them onto your home screen. To organize further, **create folders** by dragging one app on top of another. This will help you stay organized, especially if you have many apps.

○ You can also change the **icon size** under **Settings** to make your apps easier to tap, particularly if you prefer larger icons.

4. Set Up Google Assistant

○ Google Assistant is your voice-activated helper. To set it up, **go to Settings > Google > Search, Assistant & Voice**. Turn on the **Assistant**, then follow the prompts to **train your voice** so that Google Assistant recognizes your commands. You can ask it to set reminders, make calls, or even control smart home devices.

○ You can also change the **Assistant's voice** and **language preferences** to suit your needs.

5. Add Widgets to Your Home Screen

○ Widgets allow you to see important information at a glance, like the weather or calendar events, directly from your home screen. To add a widget, **tap and hold** on the home screen, then select **"Widgets"**.

Choose the widgets you want to add and drag them to your desired location.

- Popular widgets include **Google Calendar**, **Google Keep**, **Weather**, and **Clock**.

6. **Customize Your Ringtones and Notifications**

- Personalize your phone's **ringer** and **notification sounds** by going to **Settings > Sound & Vibration**. Here, you can select a **new ringtone** for calls and customize notification sounds for messages, emails, and apps.

- You can also turn on **vibration patterns** or set **Do Not Disturb** preferences for specific times or events.

7. Enable Accessibility Features

- If you prefer larger text or need additional accessibility tools, head to **Settings > Accessibility**. You can adjust text size, enable **magnification gestures**, or turn on **color correction** for better visibility. These features are particularly helpful for seniors or anyone who needs extra support with their device.

8. Set Up Screen Lock and Security Preferences

- To protect your data, it's essential to set up a **screen lock**. Choose from **PIN, pattern, password**, or **biometric options** like **fingerprint or Face Unlock**. Go to **Settings > Security** to set up your preferred method.

- You can also enable **Find My Device** here, which helps you locate your phone if it's lost.

Chapter 3

Mastering the Basics

3.1 Navigating the Interface with Ease

Navigating the **Google Pixel 9a** interface is simple and intuitive, designed to make your smartphone experience smooth and efficient. Whether you're new to smartphones or just switching to a Pixel, you'll find the layout easy to understand. Here's a quick guide to get you comfortable with the basic navigation:

1. **Home   Screen**
   The **Home screen** is the starting point for most of your activities. It's where you'll find your **apps**, **widgets**, and **shortcuts** to key features. You can swipe left or right to view additional home screens, and you can **customize** these screens by adding or removing apps and widgets.

   ○ **Accessing Apps**: To open apps, simply **tap** on their icons. To organize apps, you can drag them into **folders** by dragging one app on top of another.

- ○ **Using the Google Search Bar**: The search bar at the top of your Home screen lets you search the web, apps, or even your device. Tap the search bar, type your query, or activate **Google Assistant** by saying, "Hey Google."

2. **Navigation   Bar**

The **navigation bar** at the bottom of the screen gives you quick access to essential functions:

- ○ **Home**: The **circle** icon takes you back to the Home screen from any app.

- ○ **Back**: The **triangle** icon lets you go back to the previous screen or step within   an   app.

- ○ **Recent Apps**: The **square** icon shows your recent apps. Tap it to see what you've been using recently, and swipe up on an app to close it.

3. You can also use **gesture navigation** for a cleaner look. To activate gestures:

○ **Go to Settings > System > Gestures > Swipe Up on Home Button** to turn on gesture navigation.

○ **Swiping Up**: From the Home screen, swipe up to access your apps.

○ **Swiping Left or Right**: Switch between apps or go back to previous screens with a swipe.

4. **Quick Settings Menu**
Swipe **down** from the top of the screen to access the **Quick Settings menu**. This panel lets you quickly toggle settings like:

○ **Wi-Fi** and **Bluetooth**: Turn these on or off.

- **Do Not Disturb**: Mute calls and notifications temporarily.

- **Battery Saver**: Turn on to extend battery life.

- **Screen Brightness**: Adjust brightness for better visibility.

5. You can also access additional settings by tapping the **gear icon** in the top right corner to open the **full Settings menu**.

6. **Notifications**
   Notifications alert you to messages, updates, and apps. You can view them by swiping **down** from the top of the screen.

   - **Manage Notifications**: To clear notifications, swipe them away. To open them, tap on the notification for more details or to interact with it.

○ **App Notifications**: You can adjust how notifications appear by going to **Settings > Apps & Notifications** and selecting your preferences.

7. **App Drawer**

To access all the apps installed on your device, swipe **up** from the Home screen. The **App Drawer** will show all your apps in alphabetical order. Here you can scroll through, search for apps, or organize them as needed.

8. **App Shortcuts and Widgets**

For quick access to features, you can add **widgets** to your Home screen. Widgets are small, interactive versions of apps that display information or give you access to specific features.

○ **Adding Widgets**: Tap and hold on the home screen, then tap **Widgets**. Choose the widget you want and drag it to your Home screen.

○ **App Shortcuts**: Some apps have shortcuts to specific actions (e.g., opening a camera in portrait mode). Tap and hold the app icon to see available   shortcuts.

3.2 Essential Features for Daily Use

Your **Google Pixel 9a** is packed with powerful features that make daily tasks easier, more efficient, and enjoyable. Whether you're managing notifications, capturing photos, or keeping your device secure, these essential features will help you get the most out of your phone every day. Here's a breakdown of the must-have features for daily use:

1. **Google   Assistant**
   Google Assistant is your **voice-activated helper**. It can handle tasks, answer questions, and make suggestions, all hands-free. Here's how to use it:

   ○ **Activate Google Assistant**: Say, **"Hey Google"** or **press and hold** the Home   button.

   ○ **What Google Assistant Can Do**: You can ask it to set reminders, send texts, make calls, play music, and even control your smart home devices.

- ○ **Personalization**: Go to **Settings > Google > Search, Assistant & Voice** to customize your Assistant, including changing its voice, setting routines, and managing preferences.

2. **Notifications and Do Not Disturb** Notifications keep you updated on what's happening, from new messages to important alerts. You can manage these to stay organized:

  - ○ **View Notifications**: Swipe **down** from the top of the screen to view your notifications. Tap a notification to open the app or take action.

  - ○ **Clear Notifications**: Swipe away notifications to clear them or tap the **gear icon** for more options.

  - ○ **Do Not Disturb Mode**: When you need a break, turn on **Do Not Disturb** from the Quick Settings menu (swipe down from the top). You can adjust what's allowed during Do Not Disturb, such as calls from specific contacts.

3. Camera   Features

The **Pixel 9a's camera** is one of its standout features, delivering high-quality photos with just a tap. These essential camera features will help you capture moments   effortlessly:

- ○ **Quick Launch Camera**: Double press the **power button** to open the camera instantly, even if your phone is locked.

- ○ **Night Sight**: Capture bright, clear photos even in low light. Simply open the camera and swipe to **Night Sight** mode for stunning results in the dark.

- ○ **Portrait Mode**: Blur the background and focus on your subject for professional-looking portraits.

- **Google Lens**: Use Google Lens to identify objects, translate text, or scan QR codes directly from the camera.

4. **Battery Saver and Charging**
Your Pixel 9a's battery is designed to last throughout the day. Here's how to maximize its life:

- **Battery Saver Mode**: If you're running low on battery, turn on **Battery Saver** from the Quick Settings menu. This reduces background activity and helps extend battery life.

- **Adaptive Battery**: Pixel 9a learns your usage habits and optimizes battery consumption. This feature is automatically turned on, but you can manage it by going to **Settings > Battery**.

○ **Fast Charging**: Use the included **18W USB-C charger** to quickly charge your phone. Plug it in, and your device will power up in no time.

5. App   Management

Keeping your apps organized and efficient is key to a smooth daily experience:

○ **App Drawer**: Swipe **up** from the home screen to access all your installed apps. Use the **search bar** at the top to find apps quickly.

○ **App Shortcuts**: Press and hold an app icon to reveal **shortcuts** to specific app features, like composing a new email or starting a workout.

○ **App Notifications**: Manage individual app notifications in **Settings > Apps & Notifications**. You can set preferences for each app, including which notifications you want to receive and how they appear.

6. Security   Features
Your **Pixel 9a** is packed with security features to keep your personal data safe:

○ **Fingerprint   Unlock**:   Set   up **fingerprint recognition** to unlock your phone securely and quickly. Go to **Settings > Security > Fingerprint** to   set   it   up.

○ **Face Unlock**: Alternatively, set up **Face Unlock** for convenient face recognition to unlock your phone.

○ **Find My Device**: If your phone is ever lost, you can track its location or remotely wipe it through **Find My Device** in **Settings > Security**.

7. **Google Photos and Cloud Backup**
Back up your data to keep everything safe,

even if you lose your device:

- Google Photos: Your photos and videos automatically sync to Google Photos, so you'll never lose memories. You can access them from any device by signing into your Google account.

- Cloud Backup: Enable Google One or Google Drive to back up app data, settings, and contacts, ensuring your information is always secure and accessible.

8. Google Play Store
The Google Play Store is your go-to place for downloading apps, games, and media:

- Explore New Apps: Open the Play Store, tap the Search bar, and browse new or popular apps.

- App Updates: Keep your apps up to date by going to My Apps & Games in the Play Store to check for updates.

3.3 Customizing Settings for Your Needs

One of the best things about the **Google Pixel 9a** is how easily you can personalize it to suit your lifestyle. Whether you want to adjust the **display**, **notifications**, or **privacy settings**, the **Pixel 9a** gives you the flexibility to make your phone work the way you do. Here's a quick guide on how to customize your settings to match your preferences:

1. **Display**   **Settings**

   o **Brightness**: Adjust the screen brightness to suit your environment. Swipe down from the top of the screen to access the **Quick Settings** and use the **brightness slider**. You can also turn on **Adaptive Brightness** to have your phone automatically adjust brightness based on your surroundings.

   o **Dark Mode**: For a more comfortable viewing experience, especially in low light, switch to **Dark Mode**. Go to **Settings > Display** and toggle **Dark Theme** on. It's easier on the eyes and can also help save battery life.

○ **Screen Timeout**: To extend battery life or keep the screen on longer, adjust the screen timeout. Go to **Settings > Display > Sleep** and select how long you want the screen to stay active when not in use.

○ **Font Size and Display Size**: If you need larger text or icons, go to **Settings > Display > Font Size** and **Display Size**. Here, you can make text larger for easier reading or adjust the screen layout to suit your needs.

2. **Sound and Vibration Settings**

○ **Ringtones and Notification Sounds**: Customize your ringtone by going to **Settings > Sound & Vibration > Phone Ringtone**. You can choose from a variety of built-in ringtones or even set a song from your library as your ringtone.

- o **Volume Controls**: Adjust the volume for **calls, media, alarms**, and **notifications** separately. Go to **Settings > Sound & Vibration** to manage individual volume sliders.

- o **Vibration Settings**: If you prefer your phone to vibrate instead of ringing, you can adjust vibration patterns for incoming calls and notifications by going to **Settings > Sound & Vibration > Vibration**.

3. Notifications

- o **Manage App Notifications**: If certain apps are sending too many notifications, you can customize how and when they appear. Go to **Settings > Apps & Notifications > Notifications**. From here, you can choose to turn off, limit, or prioritize notifications for specific apps.

- ○ **Do Not Disturb**: When you need some peace and quiet, use **Do Not Disturb** mode. You can access it quickly by swiping down from the top of the screen and tapping the **Do Not Disturb** icon. For more control, go to **Settings > Sound & Vibration > Do Not Disturb** to set schedules or allow calls from certain contacts.

4. Privacy and Security Settings

- ○ **Fingerprint and Face Unlock**: To ensure your phone is secure yet easy to unlock, set up **fingerprint recognition** or **Face Unlock**. Go to **Settings > Security** to set up one or both options. This makes unlocking your phone faster and more secure.

- ○ **App Permissions**: Control which apps have access to sensitive information, like your **camera**, **location**, or **microphone**. Go to **Settings > Apps & Notifications > App Permissions** and manage access for each app.

○ **Find My Device**: In case your phone gets lost or stolen, enable **Find My Device** to track it. Go to **Settings > Security > Find My Device** to turn on location tracking and remote locking.

5. Connectivity   Settings

○ **Wi-Fi and Bluetooth**: Easily manage your connections by going to **Settings > Network & Internet**. Here, you can turn **Wi-Fi** and **Bluetooth** on or off, connect to networks, or manage saved networks.

○ **Hotspot & Tethering**: If you need to share your mobile data, you can turn your Pixel 9a into a hotspot. Go to **Settings > Network & Internet >**

Hotspot & Tethering to set it up and share your connection with other devices.

- ○ **Data Saver**: To save data when using mobile internet, turn on **Data Saver** in **Settings > Network & Internet > Data Saver**. This reduces background data usage by apps.

6. **Google Account and Sync Settings**

- ○ **Account Sync**: To ensure all your data is backed up and synced across your devices, go to **Settings > Google > Sync**. Here, you can choose what to sync (contacts, calendar, Gmail, etc.) to keep everything up-to-date.

- ○ **Google Assistant**: Personalize your **Google Assistant** by going to **Settings > Google > Search, Assistant & Voice**. You can change the voice, language, and even set up **routines** to automate daily tasks (e.g., getting weather updates or turning off smart lights).

7. **Customizing the Home Screen**

○ **App Layout and Widgets**: Organize your apps by grouping them into **folders** for a cleaner layout. Tap and hold on an app icon to **move** it around or create a folder by dragging one app onto another. You can also add **widgets** to your home screen for quick access to information like the weather, calendar, or music.

○ **Icon and Grid Size**: Adjust the size of your app icons and the layout of your home screen by going to **Settings > Display > Advanced > Display Size**. You can increase the icon size or change the grid layout to fit more apps.

8. Battery and Power Settings

- **Battery Usage**: Keep track of which apps are using the most battery by going to **Settings > Battery**. You'll see a breakdown of power consumption and tips for saving battery life.

- **Adaptive Battery**: The Pixel 9a learns how you use your phone and optimizes battery life for your habits. Enable **Adaptive Battery** in **Settings > Battery** to get the most out of your device throughout the day.

Chapter 4

Unlocking the Full Potential of Your Camera

4.1 Capturing Stunning Photos with the 48MP Camera

The **Google Pixel 9a** is equipped with a powerful **48MP main camera**, allowing you to capture high-resolution, sharp images with incredible detail. Whether you're snapping a quick shot or taking a more deliberate photograph, the Pixel 9a's camera will help you take professional-quality pictures with ease. Here's how to make the most of it:

1. **Understanding the 48MP Sensor**
   The Pixel 9a's **48MP main camera** uses a large sensor to capture more detail, meaning your photos will have vivid color and sharpness even when zoomed in. The camera's **AI technology** helps improve colors, contrast, and dynamic range,

ensuring your photos look great in any lighting.

2. **Capturing Sharp, Detailed Photos**
To capture stunning photos with crisp detail, follow these tips:

- ○ **Focus on Your Subject**: Simply tap the screen to focus on your subject. The camera will automatically adjust for the best exposure and focus.

- ○ **Stay Steady**: To avoid blurry images, keep your phone steady while taking the shot. If you're capturing a still subject, you can hold the phone still for a second to ensure the shot is crisp.

- ○ **Use the Full 48MP Mode**: The Pixel 9a's camera offers a high-resolution mode for incredible detail. You can access it by tapping the **three-line menu** in the camera app and selecting **"48MP"**. This mode is perfect for capturing intricate details or large group shots where you want the clarity to stand out.

3. **Improving Lighting with Night Sight**
   Even in low-light conditions, the **Pixel 9a's Night Sight** mode excels at capturing bright and clear images. To use it:

   o Open the camera app and swipe to **Night Sight** mode.

   o Hold your phone steady while the camera gathers light for a few seconds. The Pixel 9a will use its computational photography to brighten up the image and reduce noise.

   o Night Sight works wonders in dimly lit environments, making it ideal for shooting in places like restaurants, during sunset, or at night.

4. **Portrait Mode for Beautiful Depth**
   The **Portrait Mode** is great for capturing

beautiful, professional-looking photos where your subject stands out against a soft, blurred background. Here's how to use it:

- o Switch to **Portrait Mode** in the camera app by swiping over the mode options.

- o Focus on your subject and take the shot. The Pixel 9a will automatically blur the background to give the effect of a high-quality DSLR camera.

- o For best results, ensure your subject is a few feet away from the background to create more separation.

5. **Using the AI for Color and Exposure Adjustment**
The Pixel 9a's camera has built-in **AI features** that enhance your photos in real time. It adjusts the **exposure** to ensure your images aren't too dark or overexposed and enhances **color saturation** to make your

photos look more vibrant. You don't have to do anything extra—just take the shot, and the camera's AI will do the rest.

6. **Zooming and Capturing Detail**
While the Pixel 9a doesn't have an optical zoom lens, its **digital zoom** can still capture impressive   detail:

   ○ Pinch to zoom in on your subject, but try not to go beyond **2x zoom** to maintain photo quality. For further zoom, consider getting closer to your subject.

   ○ The AI helps reduce noise and maintain sharpness, even when zooming in on a subject at a distance.

7. **Using the Timer for Steady Shots**
For group photos or self-portraits, the **self-timer** feature is a great tool. To use it:

   ○ Tap the **timer icon** in the camera app and choose a 3-second or 10-second delay.

- Set up your shot, and the camera will take the photo after the selected delay, giving you time to get into position.

8. **Editing   Photos   After   Capture**
   After taking your photo, the **Google Photos** app allows you to enhance and edit your   images:

   - **Auto-Enhance**: In the Photos app, tap the **Auto** button to apply quick adjustments to color, sharpness, and contrast.

   - **Manual Edits**: For more control, tap the **Edit** icon and adjust features like brightness,   contrast,   warmth, saturation, and sharpness. You can also crop or rotate the image and add filters.

   - **Lens Blur**: Use **Lens Blur** in the editing options to add a bokeh effect to photos taken in **Portrait Mode** or to blur the background further.

4.2 Tips for Perfect Selfies and Group Shots

The **Google Pixel 9a** is equipped with a **13MP front camera** that takes sharp, vibrant selfies and group shots. With a few simple tips, you can enhance your selfies and group pictures, ensuring they always look their best.

1. **Perfecting   Your   Selfie**

   ○ **Find the Right Lighting**: Lighting is crucial for a great selfie. Natural light works best, so position yourself near a window or outdoors. Avoid harsh direct sunlight, as it can create shadows or make your face look too bright. If you're indoors, try facing a soft light source, like a lamp or a light-colored wall, to brighten your face evenly.

   ○ **Use the Screen as a Mirror**: The front camera allows you to preview your shot before you snap it. Hold your phone at **eye level** and check your positioning. Slightly tilt your head or angle your face to get the most flattering angle. Avoid shooting from below, as it can create unflattering shadows or angles.

○ **Portrait Mode for a Softer Look**: Switch to **Portrait Mode** for a professional touch. It creates a beautiful **bokeh** effect, blurring the background and making you stand out more. This feature is perfect for selfies where you want the focus to be entirely on you.

○ **Smile Naturally**: The best selfies are the ones where you look natural and relaxed. Avoid forced or stiff smiles. A genuine smile will make your selfie appear more vibrant and approachable.

○ **Use the Timer for Steady Shots**: To avoid blurry selfies from a shaky hand, use the **self-timer** feature. Tap the **timer icon** on the screen and choose either the 3-second or 10-second option to give yourself time to pose without worrying about pressing the shutter button.

2. Tips for Great Group Shots

- ○ **Check Your Background**: Before taking a group shot, take a moment to evaluate the background. A clean, simple backdrop works best, as busy backgrounds can distract from the people in the photo. Try to avoid clutter or anything that might take attention away from the group.

- ○ **Position Everyone**: Make sure everyone is visible and arranged in a way that looks balanced. **Step back** a little to fit everyone in the frame if necessary. You can also use the **gridlines** option in the camera settings to help with alignment.

○ **Use Portrait Mode for Group Shots**: While **Portrait Mode** is typically used for individual shots, it can also be great for group photos. It subtly blurs the background, allowing your group to stand out. Just make sure everyone in the shot is within the same focal plane (i.e., facing the camera at the same distance).

○ **Capture Multiple Shots**: In a group setting, people often blink or move at the wrong moment. To ensure you get a great shot, take multiple photos in quick succession. You can always choose the best one later.

○ **Use the Wide Angle Feature**: For larger groups, the **Pixel 9a's 13MP camera** has a **wide-angle lens** that lets you fit more people into the frame. Simply zoom out or adjust the position to include everyone, making sure no one gets cut off.

- **Get Everyone to Look at the Camera**: For a more engaging group shot, ensure everyone is looking at the camera. You can ask everyone to smile at the same time, or if you want a more candid look, try capturing the moment while everyone is laughing or talking.

3. **Making the Most of the Front Camera Features**

- **AI Enhancement**: The Pixel 9a's camera uses **AI to enhance your selfies and group shots** by adjusting lighting, color balance, and contrast. This means that your photos will automatically have better color, clarity, and overall appeal, even in challenging lighting situations.

- **Adjusting the Exposure**: If the lighting isn't perfect, tap on the screen where you want the focus, and use the **exposure slider** to brighten or darken the photo. This is especially useful when the lighting is uneven or if your face appears too dark.

o **HDR for Better Detail**: High Dynamic Range (HDR) helps balance the light and dark areas of your photo. The Pixel 9a automatically uses **HDR** to make sure your selfies and group shots look balanced, with rich details and vibrant colors, even when the light is tricky.

4. **Selfie Editing and Enhancement**

o After taking your selfie or group shot, you can further enhance it using the **Google Photos** app. Use the **Auto Enhance** feature to adjust colors, sharpness, and brightness automatically. You can also manually tweak settings like **brightness**, **contrast**, and **saturation**.

○ **Filters**: If you want to add a little more flair to your photos, apply filters directly in the Google Photos app. Whether it's a simple filter or a more artistic style, filters can give your selfies and group shots a unique look.

4.3 Night Sight and Advanced Features

The **Google Pixel 9a** excels in capturing stunning images even in low-light conditions, thanks to its **Night Sight** mode and advanced camera features. Whether you're snapping photos at sunset, in dimly lit restaurants, or on a night out, the Pixel 9a ensures that your photos remain bright, clear, and detailed. Here's how to make the most of **Night Sight** and other advanced features:

1. Night Sight: Low-Light Photography Made Easy

Night Sight is one of the standout features of the Pixel 9a, allowing you to capture detailed, vibrant photos in **low-light** environments where other cameras might struggle. Here's how to use it effectively:

- **Activate Night Sight**: Open the camera app and swipe to **Night Sight** mode. If you're in a low-light environment, the camera will automatically suggest switching to Night Sight, or you can manually   select   it.

- **Hold Steady**: When taking photos in Night Sight, it's important to keep your phone as steady as possible. The longer exposure time can lead to blurry images if the phone is moving. Hold the camera still for a few seconds while it gathers light and processes the   image.

- **Capture Amazing Detail**: Night Sight works by taking multiple shots at different exposures and combining them to create a well-lit, sharp photo with minimized noise. This means that even at night, you can capture crisp details without the graininess that often appears in other low-light shots.

- **Use for Landscapes and Portraits**: Night Sight works great for both wide landscapes and close-up portrait shots, ensuring vibrant colors and sharp focus no matter what   you're   shooting.

2. Portrait Mode: Adding Depth to Your Photos

The Pixel 9a's **Portrait Mode** is another powerful tool for capturing professional-quality photos. It helps you focus on your subject while creating a **blurred background**, or **bokeh effect**, making your photos look like they were taken with an expensive DSLR camera.

- **Activate Portrait Mode**: Open the camera app and swipe to **Portrait Mode**. The camera will automatically detect faces and apply the background blur effect.

- **Adjust the Blur**: After taking your portrait photo, you can use the **Edit** function in Google Photos to adjust the blur intensity. This gives you more control over how much of the background you want to blur.

3. Super Res Zoom: Capture Clear Details from a Distance

The **Super Res Zoom** feature on the Pixel 9a allows you to zoom in on distant subjects while maintaining impressive clarity and sharpness. While the Pixel 9a doesn't have optical zoom, **Super Res Zoom** compensates by using computational photography to enhance the quality of zoomed-in images.

- **Zoom in with Confidence**: Instead of simply pinching to zoom in and risking a blurry photo, rely on the **Super Res Zoom** to enhance the detail of your zoomed-in shots without the loss of quality.

- **Optimal Zoom Range**: For the best results, try to limit the zoom to about **2x**. Anything beyond that can reduce the clarity, but within this range, the Pixel 9a's software works wonders to sharpen your image.

4. HDR+ with Bracketing: Better Exposure in Every Shot

High Dynamic Range (HDR) helps balance the light and dark areas of your photos, resulting in images with more detail and more accurate colors, especially in high-contrast scenes (like a bright sky or dark shadows).

- **How HDR+ Works**: The Pixel 9a automatically applies **HDR+** to your photos. It captures multiple images at different exposures and combines them to create a well-lit, detailed image.

- **Use HDR for Stunning Landscapes and City Shots**: When photographing landscapes or city scenes, HDR+ helps keep both the bright sky and the darker foreground in perfect balance, avoiding washed-out highlights or overly dark shadows.

5. Google Lens: A Smart, Interactive Way to Capture the World

Google Lens is an advanced feature that allows you to interact with the world around you in new ways. It uses the camera to identify objects, translate text, and even provide contextual information in real time.

- **Activate Google Lens**: Open the camera app and tap the **Google Lens** icon. Point your camera at anything you want to learn more about, like a landmark, plant, or even a   product.

- **Translate Text**: If you're traveling or encountering foreign language text, Google Lens can translate the text into your preferred language instantly. Just point the camera at the text and tap to see the translation.

- **Shop or Learn More**: You can also use Lens to find similar products online or get more information about something you're looking at. Whether it's a famous painting or an interesting item in a store, Google Lens makes it easy to explore the world.

6. Astrophotography Mode: Capture the Night Sky

For those interested in **astrophotography**, the Pixel 9a offers a special mode that allows you to take long-exposure shots of the night sky, capturing stars, planets, and even the Milky Way in stunning detail.

- **Activate Astrophotography Mode**: When you're outside at night, open the camera app and switch to **Night Sight**. Then, select the **Starry Sky** option, which will take a long exposure shot of the stars. Ensure that the phone is steady during the shot to avoid any blur.

- **Great for Clear, Starry Nights**: This feature works best on clear, dark nights when light pollution is minimal, and you're away from city lights.

7. Motion Photos: Capture the Action

The **Pixel 9a** lets you capture a moment in **motion** with **Motion Photos**. This feature takes a short video along with your still photo, so you can capture the action leading up to the shot.

- **How Motion Photos Work**: When enabled, the camera records a few seconds of video before you press the shutter button. You can view the motion in the Photos app by holding your finger on the photo. This adds a dynamic element to your photos and is perfect for capturing action shots, such as jumping, running, or a quick gesture.

8. Time Lapse and Slow Motion

For those interested in creative video options, the Pixel 9a offers both **Time Lapse** and **Slow Motion** modes.

- **Time Lapse**: Use **Time Lapse** to capture long events like sunsets or traffic in a few seconds of footage. Simply swipe to the **Time Lapse** mode in the camera app and press the record button.

- **Slow Motion**: Use **Slow Motion** to capture fast-moving moments, like a ball bouncing or a pet playing. Switch to **Slow Motion** mode and watch the action unfold in dramatic detail.

4.4 Using Google's AI to Enhance Your Photos

One of the standout features of the **Google Pixel 9a** is its ability to leverage **Google's powerful AI** to enhance your photos in ways that traditional cameras can't match. Whether you're looking to improve lighting, sharpness, or details, Google's AI does the hard work for you. Here's how you can use AI to make every shot look better:

1. AI-Powered Photography: How It Works

Google's **AI technology** automatically improves your photos in real-time. When you take a photo, the Pixel 9a's camera uses machine learning to analyze the scene, detect faces, adjust exposure, and fine-tune colors. This makes your photos look more vibrant, with better contrast and sharpness, even without needing any manual edits.

- **Automatic Adjustments**: The AI adjusts brightness, saturation, and exposure to ensure the best possible photo in varying lighting   conditions.

- **Scene Recognition**: The AI also recognizes different scenes (such as landscapes, portraits, or night shots) and adjusts the settings accordingly, making sure each photo looks natural.

2. Smart HDR+ for Improved Detail

The Pixel 9a's **HDR+** technology uses AI to improve the dynamic range of your photos, meaning it brightens shadows and controls highlights, resulting in more balanced and detailed images.

- **In High-Contrast Situations**: HDR+ helps balance a bright sky with a darker foreground, so you won't lose detail in the shadows or have an overexposed sky.

- **Enhanced Colors**: AI also boosts the vibrancy and richness of colors, making your photos pop without looking unnatural.

3. Night Sight and AI Low-Light Enhancements

Night Sight, powered by AI, is a game-changer for low-light photography. It takes multiple exposures and uses AI to reduce noise and enhance details, resulting in clear, bright photos in even the darkest environments.

- **How It Works**: When you activate **Night Sight**, the Pixel 9a takes several exposures in quick succession, combining them to produce a bright, sharp image. The AI ensures that the final image maintains natural colors and reduced grain.

- **Real-Time Feedback**: The Pixel 9a will show you a preview of your shot as you hold your phone still, and the AI adjusts as you go, ensuring the best result possible.

4. Portrait Mode with AI for Perfect Background Blur

Portrait Mode on the **Pixel 9a** uses AI to create a stunning **bokeh effect**, where the background is artistically blurred while your subject remains sharp. The AI automatically detects faces and applies the background blur, mimicking the effect of professional cameras with a shallow depth of field.

- **Edge Detection**: The AI is smart enough to recognize the edges of a person's face and hair, ensuring the background blur doesn't spill into the subject, keeping everything looking natural and clean.

- **Adjustable Blur**: After you take the photo, you can adjust the **background blur** using Google Photos, giving you control over the effect even after the shot is taken.

5. Face Retouching with AI

If you want to enhance the **faces** in your photos, the Pixel 9a uses AI to subtly brighten skin tones, reduce blemishes, and smooth features without making the image look artificial.

- **Automatic Face Enhancements**: The AI can recognize faces and automatically improve them by softening the skin and adding a natural glow, all without looking overdone.

- **Manual Adjustments**: You can manually adjust the level of retouching in **Google Photos** if you want a more customized look, ensuring your selfies and portraits are just   right.

6. Google Photos AI Editing Tools

Once your photos are captured, Google Photos gives you access to powerful editing tools powered by AI that enhance your photos even further:

- **Auto Enhance**: Tap the **Auto** button in the **Edit** menu, and Google Photos will use AI to adjust the brightness, contrast, and saturation for a more vibrant and balanced photo.

- **Suggested Edits**: Google Photos uses AI to automatically suggest edits based on the content of your photo. For example, it might suggest boosting the color in a sunset photo or brightening a dimly lit indoor shot.

- **Sky Enhancement**: AI can enhance the sky in your photos, making sunsets, clouds, and blue skies more vibrant and eye-catching. This feature is particularly useful for landscape photos, where the sky can often appear dull in standard photos.

7. Object and Text Recognition with Google Lens

Another powerful AI feature in the **Google Pixel 9a** is **Google Lens**, which uses AI to recognize objects and text in your photos.

- **Identify Objects**: If you take a picture of a plant, a famous landmark, or an interesting object, Google Lens will analyze the photo and provide information or suggestions related to that object. You can use it to identify things, find related content, or even shop for items you see.

- **Translate Text**: Point your camera at any foreign language text, and Google Lens will instantly translate it into your preferred language, making travel and foreign language communication easier.

- **Search with Photos**: You can also search for similar images or related items by simply tapping on them in the photo with Google Lens. This makes it easy to find more information about what you're capturing.

8. Super Res Zoom with AI for Better Detail

Even though the **Pixel 9a** lacks an optical zoom lens, **Super Res Zoom**, powered by AI, enhances your zoomed-in shots, making them sharp and detailed without the blurriness that typically occurs with digital zoom.

- **How It Works**: When you zoom in, the Pixel 9a's AI takes multiple shots and blends them to create a clearer, sharper image, even at a higher zoom level. This makes it easy to capture distant subjects while maintaining detail and clarity.

Chapter 5

Boosting Performance: Speed and Efficiency

5.1 Understanding the Google Tensor G4 Chip

At the heart of the **Google Pixel 9a** is the **Google Tensor G4 chip**, an advanced piece of technology that powers everything from everyday tasks to high-end features like photography, AI, and gaming. Understanding how this chip works will give you a better appreciation of the smooth and fast experience you get from your device. Here's a breakdown of what makes the **Tensor G4** special:

1. What Is the Google Tensor G4 Chip?

The **Google Tensor G4** is Google's **custom-designed system on a chip (SoC)**, created specifically to optimize performance for Pixel devices. Unlike traditional smartphone chips that rely heavily on generic processors, the

Tensor chip integrates several specialized cores that enhance both **AI performance** and **device optimization**.

- **AI and Machine Learning**: Tensor chips are designed to handle AI and machine learning tasks more efficiently than standard processors. This means everything from **photo enhancements** to **voice recognition** and **Google Assistant** works faster and more accurately on the Pixel 9a.

- **Integration**: Unlike many other smartphones that rely on separate components for processing and AI, the Tensor G4 brings **AI processing** and **graphics rendering** together on a single chip, making it more efficient. This results in faster processing speeds, lower energy consumption, and more seamless performance across various tasks.

2. Enhanced Performance for Everyday Tasks

The Tensor G4 chip delivers **impressive performance** in a variety of areas, even for basic activities like checking emails, browsing the web, or using social media apps. Here's how it impacts your day-to-day experience:

- **Faster Load Times**: Apps open quicker, websites load faster, and tasks like scrolling through your feed or navigating apps are smoother, thanks to the efficient processing power of the Tensor chip.

- **Smooth Multitasking**: With **8GB of RAM** and the Tensor chip's multi-core architecture, you can easily run multiple apps simultaneously without noticeable lag or delays. Whether you're switching between apps or using split-screen mode, the **Pixel 9a** keeps everything flowing seamlessly.

- **Battery Efficiency**: The Tensor G4 chip also contributes to better battery management. It's optimized for energy efficiency, ensuring you get more out of your phone's **5,100mAh battery** without draining it quickly during typical usage.

3. AI-Powered Photography and Camera Enhancements

One of the standout features of the **Google Pixel 9a** is its **camera system**, and the Tensor G4 chip plays a key role in making it so powerful. With its AI capabilities, the chip helps you take stunning photos and videos with ease:

- **Real-Time Image Processing**: The **Tensor G4** handles real-time image processing during your photoshoots. From improving low-light shots with **Night Sight** to automatically adjusting the exposure in HDR photos, the chip enhances the final image with minimal effort.

- **Advanced Features like Face Detection and Portrait Mode**: The chip helps improve face detection, making portrait shots more accurate and ensuring the subject stays in focus while the background is blurred. It also contributes to better **color accuracy** and **dynamic range** in your photos.

- **Video Recording**: When recording video, the **Tensor G4** enhances **stabilization**, **color processing**, and **AI-driven improvements**, ensuring that videos are smooth, crisp, and true to life.

4. Gaming Performance and Graphics

Gaming is becoming increasingly demanding on smartphones, and the **Tensor G4** is built to meet those needs without compromising performance or battery life.

- **Smooth Gameplay**: The Tensor chip's **GPU** (graphics processing unit) provides smooth rendering of high-quality graphics in games, meaning you can enjoy your favorite mobile games without lag or stuttering.

- **Low Power Consumption**: Even during extended gaming sessions, the **Tensor G4** ensures that your Pixel 9a doesn't overheat and drain the battery quickly, thanks to its efficient power management.

5. Improved Google Assistant and Voice Recognition

With the **Tensor G4**, the **Google Pixel 9a** takes **voice interactions** and **Google Assistant** to the next level:

- **Faster Voice Recognition**: The chip enables faster **speech-to-text** processing, meaning you can dictate messages, ask questions, or set reminders with less delay.

- **Improved On-Device Processing**: Google Assistant's responses are faster, and on-device voice recognition works seamlessly without having to rely heavily on the cloud, which also improves privacy.

- **Localized AI**: The Tensor G4 makes it easier for Google Assistant to understand **regional accents** or **contextual requests**, further improving voice commands and personalizing your experience.

6. Security and Privacy Features

The **Tensor G4** chip also integrates specialized **security** features, ensuring that your data is protected while also improving the performance of **Face Unlock** and **Fingerprint Recognition**.

- **On-Device Security**: With the **Titan M2 Security Chip** built into the Tensor G4, your **passwords**, **PINs**, and **biometric data** are stored securely on your device, ensuring a high level of privacy.

- **AI-Driven Threat Detection**: The chip enhances the ability to detect **malicious activity** and **unauthorized access**, providing an extra layer of security without sacrificing device performance.

5.2 Managing Apps for Seamless Multitasking

One of the key benefits of the **Google Pixel 9a** is its ability to handle multiple tasks at once without slowing down. Thanks to the **Google Tensor G4 chip** and **8GB of RAM**, multitasking is fast, smooth, and efficient. Here's how you can manage apps effectively to ensure your Pixel 9a performs at its best while you switch between tasks with ease:

1. Understanding How Multitasking Works on Pixel 9a

The **Google Pixel 9a** is designed to make multitasking simple. The device allows you to run several apps at once, switch between them quickly, and keep them open without losing progress. The **Tensor G4 chip** optimizes background processes, so your apps run seamlessly without taking up too much power or slowing down the phone.

- **RAM Management**: With **8GB of RAM**, the Pixel 9a keeps apps in memory longer, meaning you can switch between apps quickly without having to reload them each time. It also intelligently closes unused apps to free up memory, improving performance without draining your battery.

- **App Hibernation**: When you stop using an app for a long time, the Pixel 9a automatically hibernates it, freeing up resources for the apps you're currently using. This helps maintain speed without wasting memory on unused apps.

2. Switching Between Apps with Ease

Switching between apps should be a smooth, seamless process. Here's how you can navigate quickly between open apps:

- **Recent Apps Button**: Tap the **square icon** in the navigation bar to open the **Recent Apps** screen. Here you can quickly access the apps you've used recently and switch between them with a simple tap.

- **Swipe Gestures**: If you've enabled **gesture navigation**, swipe up from the bottom of the screen to view your recent apps. You can then swipe left or right to quickly jump between open apps.

- **Close Unused Apps**: If you want to close an app completely, swipe it off the **Recent Apps** screen. However, the Pixel 9a does a great job of managing apps in the background, so closing apps manually isn't usually necessary unless you're troubleshooting or need to free up space.

3. Split-Screen Mode for Efficient Multitasking

For users who need to work with two apps at the same time, **Split-Screen Mode** is a fantastic feature. It lets you use two apps side by side, making it easier to check emails while browsing the web or take notes while watching a video.

- **How to Use Split-Screen Mode**:

  1. Open the **Recent Apps** screen.

  2. Find the app you want to use in split-screen mode and tap the **three-dot menu** at the top of the app preview.

  3. Select **"Split Screen"** from the options.

  4. Choose a second app from your recent apps or the app drawer to open in the lower half of the screen.

- **Adjusting the Split Screen**: You can adjust the size of the windows by dragging the divider up or down. This lets you allocate more space to the app you're using most, while still keeping the second app visible.

4. Managing Notifications Without Disruption

The **Google Pixel 9a** gives you the ability to stay on top of your notifications without interrupting your workflow. You can manage notifications in ways that suit your multitasking needs:

- **Quick Reply**: When you receive a message, you can reply without leaving the app you're using. Simply swipe down to open the **notification shade**, and tap **"Reply"** on the message you want to respond to.

- **Notification Prioritization**: Go to **Settings > Apps & Notifications > Notifications** to choose how you want different types of notifications to behave. You can set some apps to show **pop-up notifications** for important messages, while others can be silenced.

- **Do Not Disturb Mode**: If you need uninterrupted focus, you can turn on **Do**

Not Disturb mode, which silences all notifications (except for the ones you've allowed, such as calls from important contacts).

5. Managing Background Apps to Improve Performance

To keep your **Pixel 9a** running smoothly, it's important to manage background apps and processes:

- **Background App Limits**: Some apps continue running in the background, consuming resources and draining your battery. Go to **Settings > Battery** to see which apps are using the most power in the background. If needed, you can restrict these apps from running in the background.

- **App Permissions**: Review app permissions by going to **Settings > Apps & Notifications > App Permissions**. You can restrict background processes for apps that don't need constant access to things like **location** or **storage**, which can improve   performance.

- **Battery Saver Mode**: When your battery is running low, you can activate **Battery Saver Mode** from the **Quick Settings** menu. This feature reduces background activity and adjusts performance to extend battery   life.

6. Using Google's AI for Smarter Multitasking

The **Tensor G4 chip** enhances multitasking by using **AI** to optimize how apps run in the background. This means the Pixel 9a knows which apps you use most frequently and keeps them active, while apps you don't use as often are automatically hibernated to save power.

- **App Suggestions**: The Pixel 9a's AI can recommend apps you may need based on your habits. For example, if you're heading to work, the phone may suggest opening your calendar or email app. These smart suggestions help streamline your workflow and make multitasking more efficient.

7. Clearing Cache for Better Performance

Sometimes, apps and services can accumulate **cached data**, which may slow down performance over time. You can clear the cache to free up space and improve speed:

- **How to Clear Cache**: Go to **Settings > Storage** and tap on **Cached Data**. Here, you can clear the cache for specific apps or all apps at once, freeing up valuable storage space and improving performance.

5.3 Running Apps Smoothly with 8GB RAM

The **Google Pixel 9a** is designed to handle your daily tasks, whether you're using a single app or multitasking with multiple open at once. With **8GB of RAM**, the device delivers excellent performance, ensuring apps run smoothly, switching between them is seamless, and you don't have to worry about lag or crashes. Here's how the **8GB of RAM** helps keep your apps running smoothly:

1. What Is RAM and Why Does It Matter?

RAM (Random Access Memory) is the temporary memory that your phone uses to run apps and processes. The more RAM you have, the more tasks your device can handle at once without slowing down. With **8GB of RAM**, the Pixel 9a is well-equipped to handle a variety of apps simultaneously while maintaining fast performance.

- **Multiple Apps at Once**: With 8GB of RAM, the Pixel 9a can keep multiple apps open in the background without needing to reload them when you switch between them. Whether you're switching between a few apps or multitasking with several, the 8GB RAM ensures that everything runs smoothly without slowing down.

- **Faster App Launches**: Apps open and load faster since there's more memory available to keep data readily accessible for the tasks you're working on. You won't have to wait long for apps to start, and even large, resource-heavy apps will run without issues.

2. Efficient Multitasking

Multitasking is where **8GB of RAM** truly shines. With so many apps constantly running in the background, it's easy for a phone to get bogged down. However, the **Pixel 9a's** 8GB of RAM is optimized to handle multiple apps without any noticeable lag or slowdown.

- **Quick App Switching**: Thanks to the ample RAM, switching between apps is nearly instant. You can jump from texting in one app to checking an email and then open a web browser, all without having to wait for the app to reload or buffer.

- **Smooth Gaming and Media Consumption**: The **8GB RAM** also allows for smooth gameplay and media streaming. Whether you're playing graphic-intensive games or watching high-definition videos, you won't experience lag, stutter, or crashes. The **GPU** and **AI-powered optimizations** work together with the RAM to ensure that media runs fluidly.

3. Intelligent RAM Management

With **Google's Tensor G4 chip** and **AI enhancements**, the Pixel 9a is able to manage RAM intelligently to ensure efficiency:

- **Adaptive RAM Management**: The Pixel 9a doesn't just let apps run in the background—it also makes sure that apps which you use most frequently are kept in the active memory, so they're ready to use the moment you need them. Apps that you rarely use will be paused or unloaded to free up RAM for the active ones, keeping your phone running at its best.

- **Background App Optimization**: If you're not using certain apps, the Pixel 9a's RAM management system automatically pauses or puts them to sleep. This helps conserve both memory and battery life, ensuring you get the most out of your phone throughout the day.

4. Running Heavy Apps and Tasks Smoothly

The **Pixel 9a** doesn't just handle basic tasks well—it also performs impressively with heavy apps and tasks like:

- **Editing Photos and Videos**: With apps like **Google Photos** or **Adobe Lightroom**, you can work on high-resolution images and videos without worrying about lag or crashes. The 8GB of RAM keeps these apps running smoothly, even when you're working with large files.

- **Productivity Apps**: Whether you're using a suite of office apps, video conferencing apps like **Zoom**, or managing multiple email accounts, the Pixel 9a keeps everything running efficiently. You can compose documents, work on spreadsheets, and switch between tasks without feeling slowed down.

5. Managing RAM for Optimal Performance

If you want to ensure that the **8GB RAM** is being used as efficiently as possible, here are some tips to optimize performance:

- **Clear Recent Apps**: While the Pixel 9a does a great job of managing apps in the background, clearing recent apps can help free up memory. Swipe up from the bottom and swipe away apps you're no longer using. This can help improve performance, especially if you notice your device slowing down after running many apps at once.

- **Monitor RAM Usage**: You can check how much RAM your apps are using by going to **Settings** > **Storage** and tapping on **Memory**. If you notice any apps consuming excessive amounts of memory, you can force close them or manage their settings to improve performance.

- **Limit Background Processes**: For even better efficiency, go to **Settings** > **Developer Options** (if enabled) and adjust the **background process limit**. Reducing the number of background processes will conserve RAM and prevent apps from running unnecessarily.

6. Optimizing Battery with 8GB RAM

While the **8GB RAM** allows for smooth multitasking, it's also optimized to minimize battery drain. The **Pixel 9a** uses its memory and

AI to prioritize active apps and conserve energy by hibernating unused ones.

- **Battery Saver Mode**: If you're running low on power, activate **Battery Saver Mode** from the Quick Settings menu. This limits background activity and app refresh rates, which conserves both RAM and battery life.

- **Adaptive Battery**: The Pixel 9a uses **Adaptive Battery** technology to learn your habits and prioritize battery usage for apps you use most frequently, ensuring that power is directed toward your most important tasks.

7. Freeing Up RAM and Improving Performance

If you want to free up memory and improve performance, you can clear the **cache** for apps that store large amounts of temporary data:

- **Clear Cache**: Go to **Settings > Storage > Cached Data** to clear the cache for all apps, which can help improve both performance and available memory.

The **8GB of RAM** in your **Google Pixel 9a** ensures that apps run smoothly, multitasking is effortless, and your phone performs well, even when you're juggling multiple tasks. Whether you're running heavy apps, editing photos, or playing games, this ample RAM ensures you can do it all without slowdown. Combined with intelligent management and the powerful **Tensor G4 chip**, the Pixel 9a provides a fluid and responsive experience every time you pick up your phone.

Chapter 6

Maximizing Battery Life

6.1 How to Make the Most of Your 5,100mAh Battery

The Google Pixel 9a is equipped with a 5,100mAh battery, which offers impressive battery life that can easily get you through a full day of use. However, to ensure your device runs at its peak and lasts as long as possible, it's essential to follow a few tips to maximize the battery life. Here's how to make the most of the 5,100mAh battery:

1. Enable Battery Saver Mode

When your battery is running low, turning on Battery Saver Mode can help extend its life by limiting certain functions. It reduces background activity, notifications, and app refreshes to minimize power usage.

- How to Turn On Battery Saver Mode: Swipe down from the top of the screen to access the Quick Settings menu, then tap the Battery Saver icon to turn it on. You can also go to Settings > Battery and toggle on Battery   Saver.

- Battery Saver Customization: You can set Battery Saver to activate automatically when your battery hits a certain percentage, such   as   15%   or   5%.

2. Use Adaptive Battery

The Adaptive Battery feature helps to optimize power consumption based on your usage patterns. It prioritizes apps you use the most, reducing battery usage from apps you rarely open.

- How to Enable Adaptive Battery: Go to Settings > Battery > Adaptive Battery and toggle it on. The phone will learn your habits over time, ensuring that energy is focused on the apps and tasks you use the most.

3. Manage Screen Brightness

Screen brightness is one of the biggest battery drainers. Fortunately, you can control it to save power without sacrificing visibility.

- Automatic Brightness: Turn on Adaptive Brightness so the screen automatically adjusts brightness based on your environment and usage. This helps reduce power consumption in darker settings.

- Manual Brightness: If you prefer to control brightness manually, swipe down from the top of the screen to adjust the brightness slider. Lower the brightness when you're in a dimly lit area to save battery.

4. Limit Background Processes

Apps running in the background can drain your battery by using data, refreshing content, or sending notifications.

- Close Unused Apps: Use the Recent Apps button to swipe away apps you're not currently using. This helps to reduce the number of background processes and improves battery efficiency.

- Restrict Background Activity: Go to Settings > Apps & Notifications > Apps and select apps that you don't need running in the background. Under Battery, you can toggle off background activity for these apps.

5. Reduce Screen Timeout

The longer your screen stays on without interaction, the more battery it uses. Reducing the screen timeout can help conserve energy.

- How to Adjust Screen Timeout: Go to Settings > Display > Sleep and select a shorter timeout duration, like 30 seconds or 1 minute.

6. Turn Off Unused Features

There are certain features on the Pixel 9a that use up battery power, especially when they're not in use.

- Bluetooth and Wi-Fi: If you're not using Bluetooth or Wi-Fi, turn them off to save battery. You can easily toggle these features from the Quick Settings menu.

- Location Services: If you're not using location-based apps, turn off Location Services. Go to Settings > Location and toggle it off, or customize app permissions to limit location access.

- Vibration: If you don't need vibration for notifications, switch it off under Settings > Sound & Vibration.

7. Monitor Battery Usage

Keeping track of your battery usage can help you identify which apps or services are draining your power the most.

- How to View Battery Usage: Go to Settings > Battery > Battery Usage. This will show you which apps are using the most power, so you can decide whether to reduce usage or find alternatives.

8. Optimize Data Usage

Background data consumption by apps can also drain your battery.

- Limit Background Data: Go to Settings > Network & Internet > Data Usage and enable Data Saver. This will limit background data usage, which in turn helps conserve battery.

- Turn Off Auto-Sync: Disable auto-sync for apps that don't need constant updates. Go to Settings > Accounts and select the account to manage sync settings.

6.2 Charging Tips: Wired and Wireless

The Google Pixel 9a supports both wired and wireless charging, making it convenient for different charging setups. Here are some helpful charging tips to keep your phone powered up efficiently while preserving battery health.

1. Fast Charging with the Wired Charger

The Pixel 9a supports 18W fast charging, allowing you to quickly charge your phone when you're in a hurry.

- Using the Included Charger: Use the USB-C to USB-C cable and 18W charger that comes with your Pixel 9a for the fastest charging speeds. Plug the cable into the charging port on your device, and you'll notice your phone charging quickly.

- Charging Speed: When using the 18W charger, the Pixel 9a will charge from 0% to 50% in about 30 minutes. Always use the official charging accessories for optimal charging   performance.

2. Wireless Charging for Convenience

While the Pixel 9a doesn't support ultra-fast wireless charging, it does support 7.5W wireless charging, which is perfect for when you want a cable-free charging experience.

- How to Use Wireless Charging: Simply place your Pixel 9a on a Qi-compatible wireless charging pad. Make sure the phone is properly aligned on the pad to ensure efficient charging. Wireless charging is slower than wired charging, but it's great for overnight charging or when you're working at your desk.

- Optimal Charging Conditions: For efficient wireless charging, ensure that your charging pad is not obstructed and is on a flat, stable surface. If you use a phone case, it should be thin and non-metallic to avoid interference with the charging process.

3. Charging Habits to Preserve Battery Life

To preserve the long-term health of your Pixel 9a's battery, it's important to adopt healthy charging habits. Here are a few best practices:

- Avoid Overcharging: It's best to unplug your device once it reaches 100% to prevent overcharging. The Pixel 9a has built-in features that help prevent overcharging, but it's still good practice to unplug once fully charged.

- Avoid Charging to 0%: Try not to let your battery drain completely to 0%. Lithium-ion batteries, like the one in your Pixel 9a, perform best when charged between 20% and 80%. Regularly charging to 100% isn't as important as keeping the battery in a moderate range.

- Use Battery Saver During Charging: If you want to speed up charging, especially when your phone is in use, turn on Battery Saver Mode. This will reduce background activity, allowing the phone to charge more quickly.

4. Wireless Charging While Using Your Phone

While wireless charging is convenient, it can generate some heat. To prevent excessive heat buildup, avoid heavy tasks like gaming or streaming while the phone is on the charger. It's best to keep your phone on the charging pad and let it charge passively when you're not using it for resource-heavy tasks.

5. Charging at Night

If you leave your phone charging overnight, consider using a smart charger or charger with a timer that stops charging once the battery is full. This can help prevent the battery from staying at

100% for too long, which can improve long-term battery health.

6.3 Extending Battery Life with Power-Saving Features

The **Google Pixel 9a** is equipped with a **5,100mAh battery**, providing plenty of power for daily use. However, there are times when you may need to extend battery life, especially if you're away from a charger. Fortunately, the Pixel 9a includes a range of **power-saving features** that can help you get the most out of your battery throughout the day. Here's how to make the most of these features:

1. Activate Battery Saver Mode

Battery Saver Mode is one of the simplest and most effective ways to extend your battery life when you need it most. When activated, it limits background activity and reduces notifications to save power.

- **How to Activate Battery Saver Mode**: Swipe down from the top of the screen to open **Quick Settings** and tap the **Battery Saver** icon. You can also go to **Settings > Battery** and toggle on **Battery Saver**. The feature will automatically limit app activity and reduce certain features, such as location tracking.

- **Automatic Activation**: You can set **Battery Saver** to activate automatically when your battery reaches a certain percentage, such as **20%** or **15%**. This ensures that you don't forget to turn it on when you're low on power.

2. Use Adaptive Battery

Adaptive Battery is a feature that learns your app usage habits and optimizes battery consumption by prioritizing the apps you use the most. It ensures that apps you don't use often aren't consuming unnecessary power in the background.

- **How to Enable Adaptive Battery**: Go to **Settings > Battery** and toggle on **Adaptive Battery**. This feature works automatically, so you don't have to manually adjust it.

- **Why It Helps**: Adaptive Battery ensures that power is reserved for the apps you actively use. Apps that you haven't used in a while will have their background activity restricted, helping preserve battery life throughout the day.

3. Reduce Screen Brightness

Your phone's screen uses a significant amount of power, especially when the brightness is set too high. By adjusting the screen brightness, you can conserve battery and make your phone last longer.

- **Automatic Brightness**: Turn on **Adaptive Brightness** so your phone can automatically adjust the screen brightness based on your environment. This way, it won't use excess power when you're in darker settings.

- **Manual Adjustment**: Swipe down from the top of the screen and adjust the **brightness slider** to lower the brightness manually when you don't need it at full brightness. Lowering the screen brightness is one of the quickest and easiest ways to save   battery.

4. Turn Off Unnecessary Connectivity Features

Certain connectivity features like **Bluetooth**, **Wi-Fi**, and **Location Services** can drain battery if they're left on when not in use.

- **Turn Off Bluetooth and Wi-Fi**: If you're not using **Bluetooth** or **Wi-Fi**, simply turn them off to save battery. You can easily toggle them off from the **Quick Settings** menu.

- **Location Services**: When you don't need GPS, turn off **Location Services**. Go to **Settings > Location** and toggle off location access for apps that don't require it.

- **Airplane Mode**: If you're not using your phone for calls or data and just want to conserve as much battery as possible, turn on **Airplane Mode**. This disables all wireless features, including cellular, Wi-Fi, and Bluetooth.

5. Limit Background Processes and App Refreshing

Apps that constantly refresh or run in the background can eat away at your battery. The Pixel 9a lets you control which apps can run in the background and update on their own.

- **Background App Management**: Go to **Settings > Apps & Notifications > See All Apps**. Choose the app you want to manage and tap on **Battery**. You can restrict the app from running in the background, which will conserve both battery and data.

- **Limit App Refresh**: You can prevent certain apps from refreshing in the background by going to **Settings > Apps & Notifications > App Info**, then selecting the app and turning off **Background Data**.

6. Use Dark Mode

The **Pixel 9a** comes with **Dark Mode**, which can help conserve battery life, especially on OLED screens like the one on the Pixel 9a. Dark Mode uses less power because it consumes less energy to display darker colors, particularly black pixels.

- **How to Enable Dark Mode**: Go to **Settings > Display** and toggle on **Dark Theme**. You can also set it to activate automatically based on the time of day (e.g., switching to Dark Mode at night).

7. Monitor Battery Usage and Optimize Apps

The Pixel 9a allows you to keep track of which apps are consuming the most battery. By monitoring and managing battery usage, you can identify apps that might need optimization or removal.

- **View Battery Usage**: Go to **Settings >
  Battery > Battery Usage** to see which
  apps and features are using the most power.
  If you notice an app that's using excessive
  battery, consider limiting its background
  activity or uninstalling it if it's not
  essential.

- **Update Apps**: Keeping apps up to date can
  also help save battery, as developers often
  release updates that optimize battery
  performance. Visit the **Google Play Store**
  to   update   apps   regularly.

8. Use Power-Intensive Features Wisely

Certain   features   like   **high-performance
gaming**, **video streaming**, and **using your
camera for extended periods** can quickly drain
your battery. If you're trying to conserve power,
use these features sparingly.

- **Lower Game Settings**: If you're playing
  games, reduce the graphical settings to a
  lower level to save battery. Most mobile

games have an option to adjust performance for longer battery life.

- **Streaming**: Streaming videos in high quality can be a major battery drainer. Lower the resolution or download videos for offline viewing when possible.

9. Enable Smart Charging (Night Charging)

If you're charging your phone overnight, consider enabling **Smart Charging**, which helps preserve battery health in the long term.

- **Smart Charging**: The Pixel 9a features **smart charging** that adapts to your charging habits. If you typically charge overnight, the phone will learn your routine and stop charging once it hits **80%** and resume charging just before you wake up, preventing prolonged exposure to 100% charge and reducing stress on the battery.

Chapter 7

Advanced Features for Power Users

7.1 Gesture Navigation: Mastering Quick Actions

Gesture navigation is a sleek and intuitive way to interact with your **Google Pixel 9a**. By replacing the traditional on-screen buttons with simple swipes, you can easily navigate your phone with one hand and speed up your workflow. Here's how to master **Gesture Navigation** and use it to its full potential:

1. What Is Gesture Navigation?

Gesture navigation allows you to interact with your phone using swipes instead of the traditional **Home**, **Back**, and **Recent Apps** buttons. With a few easy gestures, you can quickly navigate your phone, switch between apps, and even access key features.

- **The Benefits of Gesture Navigation**:

  - Cleaner screen: By removing the on-screen buttons, you gain more space to view   content.

  - Faster navigation: Swiping becomes quicker than tapping buttons, reducing the time spent switching between apps and   screens.

2. Setting Up Gesture Navigation

To enable **Gesture Navigation** on your **Pixel 9a**, follow these simple steps:

- **Go to Settings**: Open **Settings** on your device.

- **Navigate to System**: Scroll down to **System > Gestures > System Navigation**.

- **Select Gesture Navigation**: Choose the option for **"Gesture Navigation"**. Once enabled, the traditional navigation buttons will disappear, and you'll be ready to swipe your way through your phone.

3. Mastering Basic Gestures

Now that you've set up **Gesture Navigation**, here are the basic gestures that you'll use throughout the day:

- **Home** **Gesture**:

  - Swipe up from the bottom of the screen to return to the **Home screen**. This replaces the traditional **Home button**. You can also swipe up and hold to access your **app drawer**.

- **Back** **Gesture**:

  - Swipe from the left or right edge of the screen to go **back**. This replaces the **Back button**, making it easier to navigate between apps and screens.

- **Recent   Apps**:

  - Swipe up from the bottom and hold to view the **Recent Apps** screen. This shows all the apps you have open, allowing you to switch between them or swipe them away to close them.

- **Switching   Between   Apps**:

  - Swipe left or right along the bottom edge of the screen to switch between **recently used apps**. This makes multitasking much faster and more fluid.

4. Quick Access Actions with Gestures

Beyond basic navigation, **Gesture Navigation** allows you to access important actions with simple gestures:

- **Opening the Google Assistant**: Swipe diagonally from the bottom corner of your screen to quickly open **Google Assistant**.

This is an efficient way to activate your voice assistant without having to press a button.

- **App Shortcuts**: Some apps have **shortcut gestures**. For example, swipe up and hold on an app's icon to reveal **quick actions** (such as messaging a contact or starting a specific function in an app) right from the home   screen.

5. Customizing Gestures

If you prefer using different gestures, you can further customize how you interact with your **Pixel 9a**. For example:

- **Navigation Bar Settings**: Go to **Settings > System > Gestures > System Navigation** to switch back to **3-button navigation** if you prefer the traditional layout or modify gesture behavior for a more personalized experience.

6. Tips for a Smoother Experience

- **Use One-Handed Mode**: If you're navigating with one hand, swipe from the middle of the screen to activate **one-handed mode**, which adjusts the UI for easier use with your thumb.

- **Practice**: It might take some time to get used to **Gesture Navigation**, but the more you practice, the more intuitive it will feel. Give it time, and soon you'll be navigating your **Pixel 9a** effortlessly.

7.2 Using Google Assistant to Automate Your Life

Google Assistant is more than just a voice-activated search tool—it can help automate daily tasks, manage your schedule, and even control smart devices in your home. By integrating Google Assistant into your daily routine, you can save time, improve productivity, and make your life more efficient. Here's how to use **Google Assistant** to automate your life:

1. Setting Up Google Assistant

Before you can start automating tasks with **Google Assistant**, you need to ensure it's set up and ready to go:

- **Activate Google Assistant**: Go to **Settings > Google > Search, Assistant & Voice**, and make sure that **Google Assistant** is turned on. You can also activate Google Assistant by saying, "**Hey Google**" or by holding the **home button** on your Pixel 9a.

- **Personalize Assistant**: From the same settings page, you can personalize your **Google Assistant**, such as changing its voice, language, and preferred accent. You can also set up routines and shortcuts to make Assistant more efficient.

2. Automating Daily Tasks with Google Assistant

Once you've set up Google Assistant, here's how to automate everyday tasks to make your life more efficient:

- **Set Routines**: Google Assistant lets you create **custom routines** to automate several tasks with one command. For example, you can create a **"Good Morning"** routine that:

    o Turns on your smart lights.

    o Reads you the weather forecast.

    o Plays your favorite playlist.

    o Reminds you of your first meeting of the day.

- To set up routines, go to **Settings > Google > Routines** and customize the actions you want to automate.

- **Create Shopping Lists and Reminders**: Simply say, **"Hey Google, add milk to my shopping list,"** and Google Assistant will add it to your shopping list in the **Google Keep** or **Google Assistant** app. You can also set reminders for tasks like appointments, meetings, or picking up groceries.

- **Control Smart Home Devices**: If you have smart devices (lights, thermostats, speakers, etc.), you can control them with **Google Assistant**. For example, "**Hey Google, turn off the lights**" or "**Hey Google, set the thermostat to 70 degrees**." You can also group devices for more efficient control, such as turning off all lights in the house with one command.

- **Manage Calendar and Events**: Google Assistant can also manage your calendar. Ask it to add events, set reminders, or provide your schedule for the day. For example, "**Hey Google, add meeting with John at 3 PM tomorrow**," and it will update your calendar accordingly.

3. Voice Commands for Hands-Free Productivity

Google Assistant allows you to complete tasks hands-free, making your phone even more convenient for when you're on the go:

- **Send Messages or Make Calls**: Instead of manually typing a message, you can simply say, "**Hey Google, send a message to Sarah**," and dictate your text. You can also initiate phone calls by saying, "**Hey Google, call Mom**."

- **Navigate Without Touching Your Phone**: Use Google Assistant for directions. Say, "**Hey Google, navigate to the nearest gas station**," and Assistant will open **Google Maps** and start guiding you.

4. Using Google Assistant for Quick Information

Google Assistant can also help you quickly find information without having to search manually:

- **Weather Updates**: **"Hey Google, what's the weather like today?"**

- **Sports Scores**: **"Hey Google, did my team win last night?"**

- **Quick Facts**: **"Hey Google, how far is it from here to New York?"**

5. Exploring More Features and Integrations

- **Multilingual Assistant**: Google Assistant can be set to understand and respond in multiple languages. This is particularly useful if you speak more than one language or want to practice a new one.

- **Assistant on Your Lock Screen**: For a more hands-free experience, you can enable **Assistant on the Lock Screen**, allowing you to use voice commands even when   your   phone   is   locked.

7.3 Exploring Hidden Features and Shortcuts

The **Google Pixel 9a** is full of hidden features and shortcuts that can make your life easier, help you work more efficiently, and offer enhanced control over your phone's settings. Here are some of the best hidden features and shortcuts to get the most out of your device:

1. Quick Screenshot

Taking a screenshot is simple, but the **Pixel 9a** has a few tricks up its sleeve for more efficient screenshots:

- **Take a Screenshot**: Press the **Power button** and the **Volume Down button** at the same time. This captures whatever is on your screen.

- **Edit After Capturing**: After you take a screenshot, a toolbar will appear at the bottom, allowing you to crop, annotate, or share the screenshot directly.

- **Scrolling Screenshot**: You can capture a scrolling screenshot by tapping **Scroll Capture** in the screenshot toolbar. This allows you to capture an entire webpage, chat, or long document in one image.

2. Screenshot with Google Assistant

Instead of using the buttons, you can take a screenshot hands-free with Google Assistant. Simply say:

- **"Hey Google, take a screenshot,"** and the Pixel 9a will instantly capture the screen and give you the option to share or edit.

3. Split-Screen Mode

The **Pixel 9a** allows you to run two apps side by side, which is perfect for multitasking:

- **Activate Split-Screen**: Open the **Recent Apps** screen and tap the **three-dot menu** on any app you want to use. Select **"Split Screen"** and choose a second app to run at the   same   time.

- **Adjust Window Size**: You can drag the divider between the apps to adjust how much screen space each one gets, making it easier   to   multitask.

4. Quick App Switching

To switch between apps quickly without going back to the Home screen, use this gesture:

- **Swipe Left or Right on the Bottom Bar**: This lets you instantly switch between your most recent apps. It's a great way to bounce between two apps with minimal effort.

5. Shake to Unfreeze

If your screen freezes or becomes unresponsive, you can **shake your phone** to automatically unfreeze it. This is a quick and convenient trick that can help when you're dealing with minor glitches.

6. Access Hidden Settings for Power Users

For advanced customization, there are **developer options** hidden within your **Pixel 9a** settings:

- **Enable Developer Options**: Go to **Settings > About phone**, then tap **Build number** 7 times to unlock **Developer Options**.

- **Developer Settings**: In **Settings > System > Developer options**, you can adjust things like **animation speed** (to make your phone feel faster), **background processes** (to limit app activity), and even **force dark mode** for apps that don't natively support it.

7. Swipe to Access Notifications and Settings

You can swipe **down** from anywhere on the screen to access **Quick Settings** and **notifications**. But did you know you can:

- **Swipe Right on the Notifications Shade** to quickly expand your **Quick Settings** for faster access to features like Wi-Fi, Bluetooth, and **Do Not Disturb**.

8. Battery Usage Stats and Optimization

Want to see exactly which apps are draining your battery? You can access detailed battery usage stats:

- **Go to Settings > Battery > Battery Usage** to see which apps and features are consuming the most power. You can also adjust settings to improve efficiency or even **restrict background activity** for high-drain apps.

7.4 Creating Routines for Maximum Productivity

Creating **routines** with **Google Assistant** allows you to automate a variety of tasks and activities, saving you time and energy. Whether you want to automate your morning routine or streamline your workday, routines can help make your day more productive.

1. Setting Up Your First Routine

Google Assistant lets you create custom routines that can automate multiple actions with a single command. Here's how to set up a basic routine:

- **Go to Settings > Google > Search, Assistant & Voice > Routines**.

- Tap **"+"** to create a new routine.

- **Choose a Trigger**: Select a command that will activate your routine, such as **"Good Morning"** or **"I'm Home"**.

- **Choose Actions**: Pick what you want Google Assistant to do when the routine is triggered. For example, you can:

- **Turn on your lights** (if you have smart lights set up).

- **Read the weather forecast**.

- **Play your favorite playlist**.

- **Set reminders** or **make calls**.

2. Predefined Routines to Save Time

Google Assistant comes with some built-in routines that can make your day easier:

- **Good Morning**: This routine can read your calendar for the day, tell you the weather, and even play your favorite music to start your day.

- **Bedtime**: When you're ready to go to sleep, the **"Good Night"** routine can set alarms, dim lights, and remind you of your schedule for the next day.

- **Leaving Home**: When you say **"I'm leaving"**, Google Assistant can turn off lights, lock doors, and even check the traffic for your commute.

3. Customizing Routines to Fit Your Lifestyle

You can fully customize routines to match your needs:

- **Morning Routine Example**:

  - Trigger: **"Good Morning"**

  - Actions: Turns on lights, reads today's weather, plays your podcast, gives reminders for your meetings, and sets your music or news.

- **Evening Routine Example**:

  - Trigger: **"Good Night"**

  - Actions: Turns off lights, sets alarms for the next day, lowers your thermostat, and plays relaxing sounds for sleep.

4. Automating Tasks for Work and Study

Google Assistant can also help automate your work and study habits:

- **Work Routine**: Set a routine that starts when you arrive at work, opening work-related apps, checking your email, and reading reminders for meetings.

- **Study Routine**: Create a routine that plays focused music, reads out your study schedule, and sets timers to ensure you stay on track with your study sessions.

5. Syncing Routines with Smart Devices

Google Assistant routines can also interact with other smart devices in your home or office. For example:

- **Smart Lights**: Automatically turn lights on or off when you enter or leave the room.

- **Thermostats**: Set the temperature when you wake up or come home, ensuring that your environment is comfortable.

6. Routines for Travel and Vacation

If you're traveling or on vacation, Google Assistant routines can help manage your itinerary and keep your day organized:

- **Travel Routine**: Set a routine to check the weather, give you the latest flight status, and even set up reminders for your packing list or meetings.

- **Vacation Routine**: When you're on vacation, automate things like turning off lights, adjusting the thermostat, and ensuring all your devices are set for energy-saving mode.

7. Review and Tweak Your Routines

Once you've set up a routine, you can review and edit it at any time to make it even more efficient:

- Go back to **Settings > Google > Routines** to modify your existing routines. You can add or remove actions, change triggers, or adjust the time when routines activate.

Chapter 8

Troubleshooting and Optimizing Your Pixel 9a

8.1 Solving Common Issues with Ease

Even the best smartphones can experience occasional hiccups. If you're encountering issues with your **Google Pixel 9a**, don't worry—there are simple solutions for many common problems. Here's a guide to help you troubleshoot and resolve issues quickly:

1. Phone Freezing or Slowing Down

If your **Pixel 9a** starts freezing or becomes sluggish, it could be due to apps running in the background, too many cached files, or a lack of available storage.

- **Restart the Phone**: A simple restart can often resolve freezing and slow performance issues. To restart your phone, press and hold the **power button**, then tap

Restart.

- **Clear Cache**: Over time, cached files can take up space and slow down performance. To clear the cache for individual apps, go to **Settings** > **Storage** > **Cached Data**. Alternatively, you can go to **Settings** > **Apps & Notifications** > **See All Apps**, select the app, and clear its cache.

- **Free Up Storage**: If your storage is almost full, it can cause slowdowns. Go to **Settings** > **Storage** to see how much space is available and remove apps, photos, or other files that are no longer needed.

2. Battery Draining Too Quickly

If you notice that your **battery is draining faster** than expected, here are some steps to fix the issue:

- **Check Battery Usage**: Go to **Settings** > **Battery** > **Battery Usage** to see which apps are consuming the most power. If an app is using excessive battery, you can restrict its background activity by going to **Settings > Apps & Notifications > See All Apps**, selecting the app, and limiting its background usage.

- **Turn Off Background Sync**: Disable background sync for apps that don't need constant updates. Go to **Settings > Accounts** and toggle off sync for apps like email or social media that constantly pull data.

- **Enable Battery Saver**: If you need to conserve battery, turn on **Battery Saver** from **Quick Settings** or go to **Settings > Battery** to enable it. This will limit background processes, reduce screen brightness, and turn off unnecessary features.

3. Wi-Fi or Bluetooth Connection Issues

Connection issues with **Wi-Fi** or **Bluetooth** can happen, but they're usually easy to fix.

- **Wi-Fi** **Issues**:

  - **Restart Your Router**: Sometimes the issue lies with your Wi-Fi network. Try restarting your router to resolve connectivity issues.

  - **Forget and Reconnect**: Go to **Settings > Network & Internet > Wi-Fi**, tap on the network you're having trouble with, then select **Forget**. Afterward, reconnect to the network by selecting it again and entering the password.

- **Bluetooth** **Issues**:

  - **Unpair and Re-pair**: If your Bluetooth device isn't connecting, go to **Settings > Bluetooth**, tap the device you're trying to connect to, and select **Forget**. Then, try reconnecting by pairing again.

○ **Check for Interference**: Make sure there are no other devices causing interference. Keep the phone close to the Bluetooth device to ensure a strong signal.

4. Screen Not Responding or Touch Issues

If your **screen is unresponsive** or experiencing touch sensitivity issues, try these fixes:

• **Clean the Screen**: Sometimes, a dirty screen can interfere with touch sensitivity. Use a microfiber cloth to gently clean your screen and remove any debris.

• **Remove Screen Protector**: If you're using a screen protector, it could be affecting the screen's responsiveness. Try removing it and check if the touch performance improves.

- **Restart the Phone**: If the screen still isn't responding, try restarting your phone to see if that resolves the issue.

5. App Crashes or Won't Open

If an app crashes or refuses to open, here's what you can do:

- **Clear App Cache**: Go to **Settings > Apps & Notifications > See All Apps**, select the app, and tap **Storage**. From there, clear the app's cache.

- **Update the App**: Make sure the app is up to date. Open the **Google Play Store**, search for the app, and check if there's an update available.

- **Reinstall the App**: If updating doesn't help, try uninstalling and reinstalling the app. This can often fix bugs or corrupted files   causing   issues.

6. No Sound or Audio Issues

If you're not hearing any sound, or if there's no audio during calls or media playback, try these fixes:

- **Check Volume Settings**: Ensure your phone's volume is turned up. Swipe down from the top of the screen to access the **Quick Settings** menu and adjust the volume slider.

- **Restart Your Phone**: Sometimes, audio issues are resolved with a simple restart. Press and hold the **power button**, and tap **Restart**.

- **Check Audio Output**: If you're using Bluetooth or wired headphones, make sure they're properly connected. If you're using Bluetooth, disconnect and reconnect the device.

7. Google Assistant Not Responding

If **Google Assistant** isn't working properly, try the following:

- **Check Settings**: Go to **Settings** > **Google** > **Search, Assistant & Voice** > **Voice**. Ensure that **Google Assistant** is turned on.

- **Retrain Voice Model**: If Google Assistant isn't recognizing your voice, you can retrain it by going to **Settings** > **Google** > **Search, Assistant & Voice** > **Voice Match** and following the prompts.

- **Check Internet Connection**: Make sure your Wi-Fi or mobile data is working properly, as Google Assistant requires an active internet connection.

8.2 Maintaining Optimal Performance

To ensure your **Pixel 9a** continues to perform optimally and efficiently over time, here are a few tips on regular maintenance and optimization:

1. Regularly Clear Cache and Unused Files

Over time, cached files and unused apps can accumulate, slowing down your device. Make it a habit to clear cache and free up storage regularly.

- **Clear App Cache**: Go to **Settings > Storage > Cached Data** and clear it. This removes temporary files that can take up space and slow down your device.

- **Uninstall Unused Apps**: If you have apps you no longer use, uninstall them to free up storage. You can check **Settings > Storage** to see how much space apps are consuming.

2. Keep Software and Apps Updated

Software and app updates often include performance improvements, bug fixes, and new features.

- **Update Your Phone**: Go to **Settings > System > Software Update** to check for system updates. Make sure your phone is running the latest version of **Android** to ensure maximum performance and security.

- **Update Apps**: Open the **Google Play Store**, tap on your profile icon, and select **Manage Apps & Devices**. From there, you can update all apps at once.

3. Manage Battery Health

Maintaining your **Pixel 9a's battery** is crucial for keeping your phone performing at its best. Follow these tips to preserve battery health:

- **Avoid Extreme Temperatures**: Keep your phone away from extreme temperatures, as both **heat** and **cold** can negatively impact battery life.

- **Enable Battery Saver**: Use **Battery Saver Mode** when your battery is low to prevent excessive power drain. This ensures that your battery lasts longer and avoids unnecessary wear.

- **Charge Smartly**: It's best to charge your phone when it hits around **20%** and unplug it around **80%**. Avoid charging to **100%** all the time, as keeping your battery at full charge for extended periods can wear it down over time.

4. Disable Unnecessary Animations

Disabling or speeding up animations can make your **Pixel 9a** feel faster and more responsive.

- **Speed Up Animations**: Enable **Developer Options** by going to **Settings > About Phone** and tapping **Build Number** 7 times. Then, go to **Settings > System > Developer Options**, and reduce or turn off the **Window Transition Scale** and **Animator Duration Scale** for faster app navigation.

5. Factory Reset for Persistent Issues

If you've tried all troubleshooting methods and your phone is still underperforming, consider performing a **factory reset**. This will restore your **Pixel 9a** to its original settings and eliminate any persistent software issues.

- **How to Perform a Factory Reset**: Go to **Settings > System > Reset** and select **Factory Data Reset**. Make sure to back up your data before doing this, as it will erase all content from the device.

8.3 Ensuring Security and Privacy

Keeping your **Google Pixel 9a** secure is essential for protecting your personal data and maintaining your privacy. Fortunately, the **Pixel 9a** offers a variety of built-in features designed to safeguard your device from unauthorized access, data breaches, and potential threats. Here's how you can ensure your phone's security and privacy are always top-notch:

1. Set Up Screen Lock and Biometric Security

The first line of defense for your **Pixel 9a** is the **screen lock**. Setting up a secure screen lock prevents unauthorized users from accessing your phone and protects your sensitive data.

- **PIN, Pattern, or Password**: You can choose between a **PIN**, **pattern**, or **password** to lock your device. A password is the most secure option, while a PIN or pattern provides quick access.

  - **How to Set a Screen Lock**: Go to **Settings > Security > Screen Lock** and choose your preferred method. Follow the on-screen instructions to complete the setup.

- **Fingerprint Unlock**: **Fingerprint recognition** is a fast and secure way to unlock your phone. Simply place your finger on the **fingerprint sensor** located at the back of your **Pixel 9a**, and it will recognize your fingerprint and unlock the device.

  - **How to Set Up Fingerprint Unlock**: Go to **Settings > Security > Fingerprint** and follow the instructions to register your fingerprint.

- **Face Unlock**: If you prefer unlocking your phone with just a glance, **Face Unlock** is another option. This uses facial recognition to unlock your device quickly.

  - **How to Set Up Face Unlock**: Go to **Settings > Security > Face Unlock** and follow the instructions to register your face.

2. Use Two-Factor Authentication (2FA)

Two-Factor Authentication (2FA) adds an extra layer of security to your accounts by requiring both your password and a verification code to access your accounts.

- **Enable 2FA for Google Accounts**: Go to **Settings > Google > Security** and select **2-Step Verification** to set it up. You can use your phone number for SMS-based codes or an authentication app like **Google Authenticator**.

- **Enable 2FA for Other Accounts**: In addition to Google, you should enable 2FA for other services like **banking apps**, **social media**, and **email**. This ensures your accounts are protected from unauthorized access.

3. Use Find My Device to Locate and Secure Your Pixel 9a

Find My Device is a handy feature that helps you locate your phone if it gets lost or stolen. It also allows you to remotely lock your phone, erase its data, or display a message for the person who finds it.

- **Enable Find My Device**: Go to **Settings > Google > Security > Find My Device**, and toggle it on. This feature allows you to track your phone's location, lock it remotely, and even erase its data if necessary.

- **Access Find My Device**: If your phone is lost, you can visit the **Find My Device** website from any browser, log in with your Google account, and see your phone's location on a map.

4. Update Software Regularly

Keeping your **Pixel 9a** updated with the latest security patches and system updates is crucial to protect it from vulnerabilities and threats. Google releases regular updates that address security issues and improve device performance.

- **How to Check for Updates**: Go to **Settings > System > Software Update** to check if there are any available updates. Make sure to install them as soon as they're available to stay protected.

- **Automatic Updates**: By default, your **Pixel 9a** will automatically download and install updates when connected to Wi-Fi. However, you can check the **Google Play Store** for app-specific updates.

5. Manage App Permissions

Granting permissions to apps helps you control what information they can access. Some apps might ask for access to sensitive data like your location, camera, or contacts. Limiting these permissions can help protect your privacy.

- **How to Manage Permissions**: Go to **Settings > Apps & Notifications > App Permissions** to review which apps have access to your data. You can disable permissions for apps that don't need access to certain information.

- **Review Permissions Regularly**: Periodically review the permissions granted to apps and remove unnecessary ones. This reduces the chances of apps collecting more data than they actually need.

6. Use a Virtual Private Network (VPN)

A **VPN** (Virtual Private Network) helps protect your data when browsing the internet, especially when using public Wi-Fi networks. A VPN encrypts your internet traffic, making it harder for third parties to access your data or track your online activity.

- **Set Up a VPN**: You can use a third-party **VPN app** from the **Google Play Store**. Once installed, follow the app's instructions to set it up and connect to a secure server.

- **When to Use a VPN**: It's especially important to use a VPN when connecting to public Wi-Fi networks, like those found in coffee shops, airports, or hotels. It adds an extra layer of protection against hackers.

7. Use Google Play Protect to Scan for Malicious Apps

Google Play Protect automatically scans your apps for any malicious behavior or vulnerabilities. It helps keep your device secure by identifying harmful apps before they can cause any damage.

- **Enable Google Play Protect**: Go to **Settings > Google > Security > Play Protect**. Here, you can check the status of your app security and perform manual scans to ensure your device is free from harmful apps.

- **App Permissions and Alerts**: If any apps are found to be risky, Google Play Protect will alert you and give you the option to remove them.

8. Encrypt Your Device for Extra Security

Device encryption ensures that all the data on your **Pixel 9a** is protected with a secure key, making it unreadable to unauthorized users. By default, the **Pixel 9a** uses full disk encryption to secure your data, but you can ensure it's enabled for maximum protection.

- **How to Encrypt Your Pixel 9a**: Go to **Settings > Security > Encryption**. Most modern phones are encrypted by default, but if you want extra reassurance, you can check that encryption is turned on.

9. Use Secure Messaging Apps

When sending sensitive information, it's important to use messaging apps that offer end-to-end encryption, ensuring your conversations are private.

- **Apps to Consider**: Use secure messaging apps like **Signal** or **WhatsApp**, which provide end-to-end encryption to protect your messages from being intercepted by hackers or unauthorized parties.

10. Protect Against Phishing and Scam Calls

Phishing and scam calls are common threats that can compromise your security. Google has built-in tools to help you identify suspicious calls and messages.

- **Call Screen**: The **Pixel 9a** comes with **Call Screen**, which allows you to screen calls from unknown numbers. Google Assistant will answer the call on your behalf and let you know if it's a scam or spam call.

- **Spam Protection**: Enable **Spam Protection** in **Settings** > **Phone** to automatically flag and block potential spam calls.

Chapter 9

Advanced Tips and Tricks

9.1 Hidden Camera Tips and Advanced Photography

The **Google Pixel 9a** offers a powerful camera system, and while it's easy to snap great photos with the basic features, there are plenty of **hidden camera tips** and **advanced photography techniques** that can help you take your photography skills to the next level. Here are some expert tips and tricks to make the most of your device's camera:

1. Use Night Sight for Stunning Low-Light Shots

One of the standout features of the **Pixel 9a** is **Night Sight**, which allows you to take bright, clear photos even in very low light conditions. It works by combining multiple exposures to capture more detail and reduce noise.

- **How to Use Night Sight**: Open the **Camera app**, swipe to **Night Sight**, and hold your phone steady for a few seconds. The camera will automatically adjust to gather more light, giving you well-lit photos in dark environments.

- **Best for**: Nighttime landscapes, indoor shots without flash, and capturing city lights.

2. Try Long Exposure for Creative Shots

Long exposure photography can create stunning effects, such as smooth waterfalls, light trails, or a starry sky. With the **Pixel 9a**, you can achieve this with ease.

- **How to Use Long Exposure**:

  1. Open the **Camera app** and select **Night Sight**.

  2. Tap on the **Settings icon** in the top-right corner and toggle on **Long**

Exposure.

3. Hold your phone steady while capturing motion, such as flowing water, cars, or moving lights.

- **Best for**: Capturing movement, like flowing water or light trails from cars.

3. Portrait Mode for Professional-Looking Photos

For beautifully blurred backgrounds (also known as **bokeh**) in your photos, use **Portrait Mode**. This mode uses **AI** to identify the subject and blur the background for a DSLR-like effect.

- **How to Use Portrait Mode**: Open the **Camera app** and swipe to **Portrait Mode**. Position your subject a few feet away from the background for the best effect.

- **Best for**: Portraits, close-ups, and isolating the subject from the background.

4. Manual Focus Control (Using Focus Peaking)

The **Pixel 9a** doesn't offer full manual control over focus, but it does include **Focus Peaking**, which highlights the areas of your shot that are in sharp focus.

- **How to Use Focus Peaking**: Open the **Camera app** in **Pro Mode** (if available), then enable **Focus Peaking** in the settings. As you adjust the focus, the areas of your shot that are in focus will be highlighted in a color (typically yellow or green).

- **Best for**: Focusing on specific details in a shot, such as macro photography or subjects at varying distances.

5. Use Google Lens for Smart Photography

Google Lens is a powerful feature that uses AI to analyze the objects in your photos. It can identify landmarks, animals, plants, and even text.

- **How to Use Google Lens**: Tap the **Google Lens icon** in the **Camera app**, point it at something you want to learn more about, and wait for Lens to analyze the image. It will provide relevant information or links related to the object.

- **Best for**: Identifying objects, translating text, or getting information about things you photograph.

6. Capture Dynamic Photos with Motion Photos

Motion Photos captures a few seconds of video before and after the photo is taken, creating a dynamic image. It's perfect for capturing moving subjects or moments that are hard to capture in just one frame.

- **How to Use Motion Photos**: In the **Camera app**, tap the **Motion Photos** icon (a small circle) at the top to activate the feature. Take your photo, and Google will capture additional frames for a dynamic effect.

- **Best for**: Capturing moments with movement, like a person jumping or a dog running.

7. Use the Timer for Perfect Selfies and Group Shots

The **self-timer** is a great tool when you want to get everyone in a shot or take a selfie without holding the phone.

- **How to Use the Timer**: Tap the **timer icon** in the Camera app and select either **3 seconds** or **10 seconds**. Get in position, and the camera will automatically take the photo when the timer ends.

- **Best for**: Group selfies, family photos, or any time you need to be in the shot.

8. Experiment with Ultra-Wide Shots (Using Google Camera's Wide-Angle Lens)

While the **Pixel 9a** doesn't come with an ultra-wide camera lens, you can still achieve a wider field of view by enabling the **Wide-Angle Lens** feature in Google Camera.

- **How to Use Wide-Angle Lens**: In the **Camera app**, swipe to **Wide Angle** mode (if available) or use a third-party camera app that supports the feature.

- **Best for**: Landscape photography, architectural shots, or wide group shots.

9.2 Keyboard Shortcuts and Time-Saving Hacks

Your **Google Pixel 9a** offers many keyboard shortcuts and time-saving tricks that can help you work faster and more efficiently. These shortcuts can be used across the operating system, from typing to navigating your apps.

Here are some of the best **keyboard shortcuts** and **hacks** to boost productivity:

1. Keyboard Shortcuts for Faster Typing

The **Pixel 9a** offers several shortcuts that make typing faster and more efficient, especially when you're typing on the **Gboard** (the default keyboard).

- **Swipe Typing**: Instead of tapping each key, use the **Swipe Typing** feature. Just **swipe across** the letters to form words instead of tapping them individually. This speeds up typing, especially when typing long texts.

- **Emoji Suggestions**: Gboard automatically suggests emojis based on your typed words. For example, typing "happy" will bring up the ☺ emoji. You can also search for emojis by typing their name.

- **One-Handed Keyboard**: To make typing easier with one hand, switch to **One-Handed Keyboard** mode. Tap the **Gboard**

icon and select the **One-Handed Keyboard** option to make the keyboard smaller and more manageable.

2. Text Expansion Shortcuts

With **Text Shortcuts**, you can type long phrases with just a few taps, saving you time when responding to messages or typing long paragraphs.

- **How to Set Up Text Shortcuts**: Go to **Settings > System > Languages & Input > Advanced > Personal Dictionary**. Tap **Add a Shortcut** and create custom shortcuts for commonly typed phrases, like your email address, phone number, or frequently used phrases (e.g., "btw" for "by the way").

3. Use the "Recents" Menu to Quickly Switch Apps

The **Recent Apps** button is one of the most powerful multitasking tools on the **Pixel 9a**. You can quickly switch between apps or even open two apps side by side using **Split-Screen Mode**.

- **How to Use Split-Screen Mode**: Swipe up from the bottom of the screen to view your recent apps. Tap the **three dots** on the top of the app you want to use, and select **Split-Screen**. Then, select the second app you want to use, and you'll have two apps running   side   by   side.

4. Use Quick Settings to Control Key Features Instantly

The **Quick Settings menu** provides easy access to frequently used features like **Wi-Fi**, **Bluetooth**, **Do Not Disturb**, and **Battery Saver**.

- **How to Access Quick Settings**: Swipe down from the top of the screen to open **Quick Settings**. You can also customize which icons appear here, ensuring that your most-used features are just one swipe away.

- **Quick Settings Tips**: Hold any icon (like **Wi-Fi** or **Bluetooth**) for quick access to its settings, saving you time when you need to make   adjustments.

5. Smart Notifications and Gestures

The **Pixel 9a** offers **smart notifications** and **gesture controls** that can help you save time when interacting with the device.

- **Smart Notifications**: The **Pixel 9a** will show you **relevant notifications** at the right time based on your schedule and usage habits. For example, you may receive traffic updates when you're getting ready to leave or reminders for upcoming appointments.

- **Gesture Controls**: Set up gestures to do things faster. For example, **double-tap** to turn on the flashlight, **swipe down** to view notifications, or **shake your phone** to take a screenshot.

6. Use Google Assistant to Save Time

Instead of manually searching for apps, contacts, or websites, use **Google Assistant** to perform tasks hands-free.

- **Launch Apps**: Say, "**Hey Google, open [app name]**" to quickly launch any app.

- **Set Reminders**: Use **Google Assistant** to set reminders or alarms by saying, "**Hey Google, remind me to call Mom at 3 PM**."

7. Screenshot Shortcut

Taking screenshots on the **Pixel 9a** is as simple as pressing the **Power button** and **Volume Down button** simultaneously. However, there's a faster way to take a screenshot with Google Assistant.

- **How to Take a Screenshot**: Just say, "**Hey Google, take a screenshot**" and the phone will instantly capture what's on your screen.

9.3 Customizing the Home Screen for Maximum Efficiency

The **Home Screen** of your **Google Pixel 9a** is where you interact with apps, widgets, and other shortcuts on a daily basis. Customizing it to suit your workflow can make your phone feel more efficient and user-friendly. Here's how you can make your **Home Screen** work smarter for you:

1. Organize Apps into Folders

Instead of scrolling through a long list of apps, group them into **folders** for better organization and quicker access.

- **How to Create a Folder**:

    1. Tap and hold an app icon on the **Home Screen**.

    2. Drag the app on top of another app to create a folder.

3. You can name the folder by tapping on the folder name and typing a custom label (e.g., **Social Media**, **Games**, **Productivity**).

- **Best for**: Grouping similar apps together to keep the Home Screen tidy and organized, such as putting all your social media apps (Facebook, Instagram, Twitter) in one folder.

2. Use Widgets for Quick Access

Widgets allow you to access information or functions from apps directly from your Home Screen without opening the app.

- **How to Add a Widget**:

    1. Tap and hold on an empty area of the **Home Screen**.

    2. Select **Widgets** from the options that appear.

3. Browse the available widgets, and drag your preferred one to the Home Screen.

- **Best for**: Adding widgets for apps you use frequently, such as **Weather**, **Calendar**, **Gmail**, or even **Google Keep** for quick note-taking.

3. Customize the App Drawer for Easy Access

The **App Drawer** is where all your apps are stored. By customizing it, you can make accessing your apps faster and more intuitive.

- **How to Organize the App Drawer**:

    1. Swipe up from the bottom of the screen to open the **App Drawer**.

    2. Tap the **three dots** in the upper-right corner and select **Sort by Alphabetical** or **Most Used** for automatic organization.

3. You can also add apps to the **Home Screen** directly from the App Drawer by dragging them onto the screen.

- **Best for**: Ensuring your most-used apps are easily accessible, without the need to search for them in the App Drawer every time.

4. Use Dynamic Wallpapers for Visual Appeal

Customizing the background of your **Home Screen** with dynamic or live wallpapers can make your phone feel more personalized.

- **How to Change Wallpaper**:

    1. Tap and hold on an empty area of the **Home Screen**.

    2. Select **Wallpaper** from the options.

    3. Choose from **Google's Wallpapers** or **Live Wallpapers**, or select your own

images.

- **Best for**: Making your phone feel more personalized with beautiful, dynamic backgrounds.

5. Prioritize Most Used Apps with the Dock

The **Dock** is the area at the bottom of the Home Screen where you can keep up to **4 apps** for easy access. Customizing it with your most-used apps allows you to reach them faster.

- **How to Customize the Dock**:

  1. Tap and hold an app from your **Home Screen**.

  2. Drag it to the **Dock** at the bottom of the screen.

- **Best for**: Keeping essential apps like **Phone**, **Messages**, **Chrome**, or your favorite social media apps at the bottom for easy   access.

6. Adjust Icon Size for Better Visibility

To make your apps easier to see, you can adjust the size of the app icons.

- **How to Change Icon Size**:

    1. Go to **Settings > Display > Advanced > Display Size**.

    2. Adjust the **icon size** slider to make the icons larger or smaller to your preference.

- **Best for**: Ensuring the icons are visible and easy to tap, especially if you have poor eyesight or prefer larger icons.

7. Set Up Quick Actions for Faster Control

Use **Quick Actions** (also known as **App Shortcuts**) to access specific features within apps directly from the **Home Screen**.

- **How to Add App Shortcuts**:

  1. Tap and hold the app icon.

  2. If the app supports Quick Actions, a list of options will appear (e.g., **Create New Event** in Calendar, **Send a Message** in WhatsApp).

  3. Select the shortcut and drag it onto your **Home Screen** for faster access.

- **Best for**: Speeding up tasks by accessing specific functions, such as sending a message, composing an email, or opening a specific playlist in music apps.

9.4 Leveraging Google's AI for Smarter Usage

Google's AI has become an integral part of the **Pixel 9a**, helping make your phone smarter and more responsive to your needs. Here are ways to leverage Google's AI to enhance your daily experience:

1. Google Assistant for Hands-Free Tasks

Google Assistant is powered by AI and can help you manage tasks, answer questions, and even control your smart home devices, all through voice commands.

- **How to Use Google Assistant**: Simply say, **"Hey Google"** or **"OK Google"** to activate it. You can ask questions, set reminders, make calls, send texts, or control your smart home gadgets without lifting a finger.

- **Best for**: Hands-free control, quick information retrieval, and automating tasks like setting alarms, getting weather updates,   and   more.

2. Smart Battery Management with AI

Your **Pixel 9a** uses AI to manage your battery life more effectively. The **Adaptive Battery** feature learns your usage habits and prioritizes battery usage for the apps you use most frequently, while limiting background activities for apps you rarely open.

- **How to Enable Adaptive Battery**: Go to **Settings > Battery > Adaptive Battery**, and toggle it on.

- **Best for**: Extending battery life by ensuring the most important apps and services get power while less-used apps consume less energy.

3. AI-Powered Image Enhancements

Google's AI works wonders in **photo editing** and enhancement. The **Pixel 9a's** camera is equipped with AI features that automatically adjust lighting, exposure, and contrast to improve your photos.

- **How to Use AI in Photos**:

  1. Open your photo in **Google Photos**.

  2. Tap **Edit**, then choose **Auto Enhance** or manually adjust the photo settings using AI-powered tools like **Color**, **Contrast**, and **Sharpness**.

- **Best for**: Improving the quality of your photos automatically without needing manual adjustments.

4. Smart Notifications and App Suggestions

Google's AI learns from your usage patterns and can prioritize notifications or suggest apps based on what you're doing or where you are. This helps you stay focused and organized.

- **How to Enable Smart Notifications**: Go to **Settings > Apps & Notifications > Notifications**, and enable **Smart Notifications**. You can also prioritize notifications from certain apps so you don't miss important updates.

- **Best for**: Reducing notification clutter by only showing you what's most important, based on your preferences and habits.

5. AI-Driven Google Lens for Smarter Interactions

Google Lens uses AI to recognize objects, text, and landmarks in real-time, providing useful information based on what it sees. It's a powerful tool for learning more about the world around you.

- **How to Use Google Lens**: Open the **Camera app** and tap the **Google Lens** icon. Point your camera at an object or text, and Google Lens will provide relevant information, translations, or shopping links.

- **Best for**: Identifying objects, translating foreign text, scanning barcodes, or finding more information about something you see.

6. AI-Based Smart Compose and Smart Replies

When typing emails, messages, or notes, **Smart Compose** and **Smart Replies** use AI to suggest complete sentences or quick responses based on the context of your conversation.

- **How to Use Smart Compose and Smart Replies**: These features are automatically enabled in apps like **Gmail** and **Messages**. As you type, suggestions will appear, and you can tap them to quickly complete your message.

- **Best for**: Speeding up typing by offering contextually relevant suggestions and responses.

7. Use AI for Travel and Traffic Updates

Google's AI-powered **Google Assistant** can help you navigate daily commutes and plan trips by providing real-time traffic updates, estimated arrival times, and smart route suggestions based on current conditions.

- **How to Use**: Ask Google, **"Hey Google, what's the traffic like to work?"** or **"Hey Google, how long will it take me to get to the airport?"** The AI will provide up-to-date traffic information and suggest the best route.

- **Best for**: Optimizing travel routes, saving time, and staying on schedule.

Chapter 10

Why the Google Pixel 9a is Perfect for You

10.1 Unbeatable Value for Beginners and Seniors

The **Google Pixel 9a** is designed with a wide range of users in mind, offering features and functionality that make it an excellent choice for both beginners and seniors. Whether you're new to smartphones or looking for a device that's easy to use and packed with essential features, the **Pixel 9a** is the perfect solution. Here's why:

1. Simple and User-Friendly Interface

The **Google Pixel 9a** runs on **pure Android**, providing a clean and intuitive user interface that's easy to navigate. Whether you're a first-time smartphone user or someone who prefers simplicity, the Pixel's design ensures that everything you need is just a tap away.

- **Home Screen Customization**: With **simple gestures** and easy access to apps, the **Pixel 9a** allows you to organize your Home Screen to suit your preferences, ensuring everything is just where you need it.

- **Large, Easy-to-Read Text**: The phone allows you to adjust the font size and display settings, making it accessible for seniors who need larger text for better visibility.

2. Streamlined Google Assistant

For those who aren't tech-savvy, the **Google Assistant** can be a game-changer. It provides hands-free control over your phone and helps you complete tasks easily. Whether you need to set reminders, send messages, or get directions, simply saying **"Hey Google"** allows you to do everything you need without having to touch your phone.

- **Voice Commands**: For beginners or seniors who may struggle with typing or navigating through apps, **Google Assistant** can make life much easier by completing tasks with simple voice commands.

3. Simple Setup Process

Setting up your **Pixel 9a** is easy and quick, thanks to Google's seamless integration and intuitive setup wizard. From **connecting to Wi-Fi** to **signing into your Google account**, the process is clear and straightforward, so you won't have to worry about complicated technical steps.

- **Onboarding for New Users**: The **Pixel 9a** guides you through every step of the setup process with clear instructions, making it beginner-friendly. Additionally, Google's **support** is readily available if you need help at any point.

4. Affordable and Reliable

The **Pixel 9a** offers exceptional value for the price. It combines an affordable price tag with premium features, such as a high-quality camera, long battery life, and fast performance. For seniors or beginners on a budget, it's a smart investment that doesn't compromise on quality.

- **Affordable**: You get an excellent smartphone experience without having to break the bank. The **Pixel 9a** is budget-friendly and delivers a premium experience at a lower price compared to other high-end devices.

10.2 How the Pixel 9a Sets Itself Apart

What makes the **Google Pixel 9a** stand out from the competition? With its unique blend of features, performance, and ease of use, the Pixel

9a sets a new standard for budget smartphones. Here's how it stands apart:

1. Stunning Camera Quality

One of the most standout features of the **Pixel 9a** is its camera. Despite being a budget-friendly device, it offers **exceptional photography capabilities**, powered by **Google's AI**.

- **High-Quality Photos**: The **48MP main camera** captures vibrant, sharp photos in all lighting conditions, from bright daylight to low-light environments, thanks to features like **Night Sight** and **HDR+**.

- **User-Friendly Camera Interface**: For beginners, the camera app is intuitive and easy to use, while still offering advanced features like **Portrait Mode** and **Motion Photos** for more experienced photographers.

2. Long-Lasting Battery Life

The **5,100mAh battery** in the **Pixel 9a** is designed to last throughout the day, even with heavy usage. With **adaptive battery technology**, it learns your usage patterns and prioritizes the apps you use most, ensuring you get the most out of every charge.

- **Battery Saver Mode**: For those who want to conserve battery, the **Battery Saver Mode** can help extend your battery life, ensuring your phone lasts even longer when you need it most.

3. Seamless Integration with Google Services

The **Pixel 9a** offers deep integration with **Google's services**, including **Google Photos**, **Google Assistant**, and **Google Drive**, providing a smooth and cohesive experience across the device.

- **Google Photos**: With **Google Photos**, you can easily store and organize your photos and videos, access them across devices, and even take advantage of the **AI-powered**

enhancements that help improve the quality of your photos.

- **Google Assistant**: The **Google Assistant** is fully integrated into the **Pixel 9a**, enabling you to get real-time information, control smart home devices, set reminders, and more—all hands-free.

4. Regular Software Updates

Unlike many budget smartphones, the **Pixel 9a** receives regular **software updates** directly from Google. This ensures that you always have access to the latest features, security patches, and system improvements.

- **No Bloatware**: The **Pixel 9a** runs on **stock Android**, so you won't encounter the bloatware that often clutters other devices, making it faster and more efficient.

5. Clean and Minimal Design

The **Pixel 9a** has a sleek and minimal design that makes it easy to hold and comfortable to use. The **6.1-inch display** strikes a perfect balance between usability and portability, and the phone's build quality is solid and durable.

- **One-Handed Use**: For seniors or anyone who prefers using their phone with one hand, the **Pixel 9a** is designed to be easy to grip and navigate.

10.3 Ready to Unlock Your Phone's Full Potential

The **Google Pixel 9a** is packed with features designed to enhance your smartphone experience, and by unlocking its full potential, you'll be able to enjoy everything it has to offer—whether you're a beginner, a senior, or an experienced user. Here's how to unlock the full potential of your **Pixel 9a**:

1. Customize Your Experience

From organizing your apps on the **Home Screen** to setting up **widgets** and **gestures**, the **Pixel 9a** is highly customizable, allowing you to tailor your phone to your personal needs and preferences.

- **Set Up Google Assistant**: Make the most of **Google Assistant** by setting it up to handle tasks like reminders, controlling smart devices, and accessing quick information   hands-free.

- **Organize Apps and Folders**: Group your apps into folders for easy access, and customize your Home Screen layout to ensure you always have the apps and features you need right at your fingertips.

2. Take Advantage of Advanced Features

Explore the **advanced camera features** such as **Night Sight**, **Portrait Mode**, and **Motion Photos** to take professional-quality photos and videos. Additionally, experiment with **gesture navigation**, **AI-powered tools**, and **Smart Routines** for enhanced functionality.

- **Google Lens**: Unlock the power of **Google Lens** to search, translate, and interact with the world around you through your camera.

- **Pro Mode in Camera**: Try **Pro Mode** for more manual control over your photos and discover how Google's AI works behind the scenes to improve your shots.

3. Make the Most of Google's Ecosystem

The **Pixel 9a** is designed to work seamlessly with other **Google devices** and services, including **Google Home**, **Google Drive**, and **Chromecast**. If you already use these services, the **Pixel 9a** can make managing your digital life even easier.

- **Google Home Integration**: Control your smart home with voice commands through **Google Assistant**, such as adjusting lights, thermostats, and more.

- **Sync Across Devices**: With **Google Drive**, your photos, documents, and data sync across your devices automatically, making it easier to access everything from anywhere.

4. Stay Secure and Private

With built-in **AI security features** like **Titan M2 Security Chip**, **Face Unlock**, and **Fingerprint Unlock**, you can keep your data secure and your phone private. Regular **security updates** ensure you're always protected from the latest threats.

- **Regular Software Updates**: The **Pixel 9a** gets timely updates directly from Google, which ensures you always have the latest features and security patches.

Conclusion

The **Google Pixel 9a** is more than just a smartphone—it's a powerful and reliable tool that adapts to your needs, whether you're just getting started with smartphones, or you're an experienced user looking for efficiency and productivity. Offering **great value**, **easy-to-use features**, and **deep Google integration**, the **Pixel 9a** stands out as the perfect device for anyone looking to unlock their phone's full potential. Whether you're capturing beautiful photos, organizing your life, or staying connected with loved ones, the **Pixel 9a** is ready to help you do it all with ease.

www.ingramcontent.com/pod-product-compliance
Lightning Source LLC
LaVergne TN
LVHW022313060326
832902LV00020B/3438